⌂ SUCCESSFUL HOME PLANS FOR THE 80's

⌂ SUCCESSFUL HOME PLANS FOR THE 80's

From Editors of Home Planners, Inc.

STRUCTURES PUBLISHING COMPANY
Farmington, Michigan 48024

Copyright © 1980 Structures Publishing Co.
24277 Indoplex Circle
Box 1002
Farmington, Michigan

Manufactured in the United States of America

Current Printing (last digit)
10 9 8 7 6 5 4 3 2 1

ISBN: 0-89999-002-9 (cloth)
      0-89999-003-7 (paper)

LIBRARY OF CONGRESS
CATALOG CARD NO.: 80-7498

Home Planners
    Successful home plans for the 80's

Farmington, Mich.: Structures Publishing

192 p.

8002   800121

Contents

Index to Designs

Cut-Out Templates

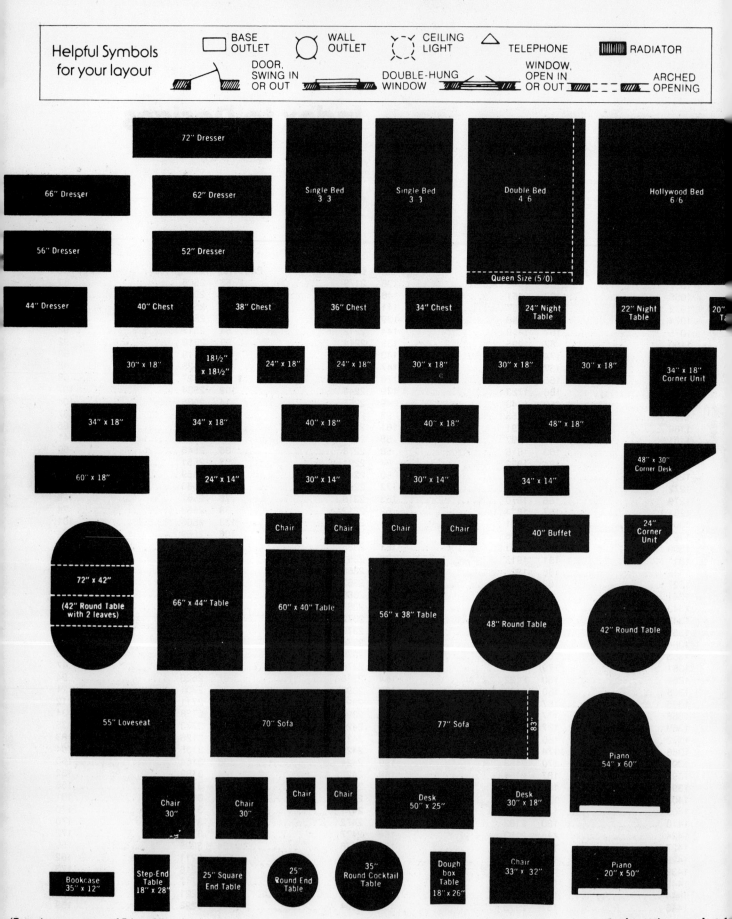

Helpful Symbols for your layout

☐ BASE OUTLET
◯ WALL OUTLET
CEILING LIGHT
△ TELEPHONE
▨ RADIATOR
DOOR, SWING IN OR OUT
DOUBLE-HUNG WINDOW
WINDOW, OPEN IN OR OUT
ARCHED OPENING

72" Dresser

66" Dresser

62" Dresser

Single Bed 3 3

Single Bed 3 3

Double Bed 4 6

Hollywood Bed 6 6

56" Dresser

52" Dresser

Queen Size (5/0)

44" Dresser

40" Chest

38" Chest

36" Chest

34" Chest

24" Night Table

22" Night Table

20" Ta

30" x 18"

18½" x 18½"

24" x 18"

24" x 18"

30" x 18"

30" x 18"

30" x 18"

34" x 18" Corner Unit

34" x 18"

34" x 18"

40" x 18"

40" x 18"

48" x 18"

48" x 30" Corner Desk

60" x 18"

24" x 14"

30" x 14"

30" x 14"

34" x 14"

24" Corner Unit

Chair

Chair

Chair

Chair

40" Buffet

72" x 42"

(42" Round Table with 2 leaves)

66" x 44" Table

60" x 40" Table

56" x 38" Table

48" Round Table

42" Round Table

55" Loveseat

70" Sofa

77" Sofa

83"

Piano 54" x 60"

Chair 30"

Chair 30"

Chair

Chair

Desk 50" x 25"

Desk 30" x 18"

Bookcase 35" x 12"

Step-End Table 18" x 28"

25" Square End Table

25" Round End Table

35" Round Cocktail Table

Dough box Table 18" x 26"

Chair 33" x 32"

Piano 20" x 50"

(Templates courtesy of Ethan Allen, Inc.)

Scale: ¼ in. equals 1 f

DESIGN CRITERIA

AVERAGE DIMENSIONS FOR MAJOR
ITEMS IN LIVING, DINING,
BEDROOMS, AND OTHER ROOMS
USED FOR LIVING.

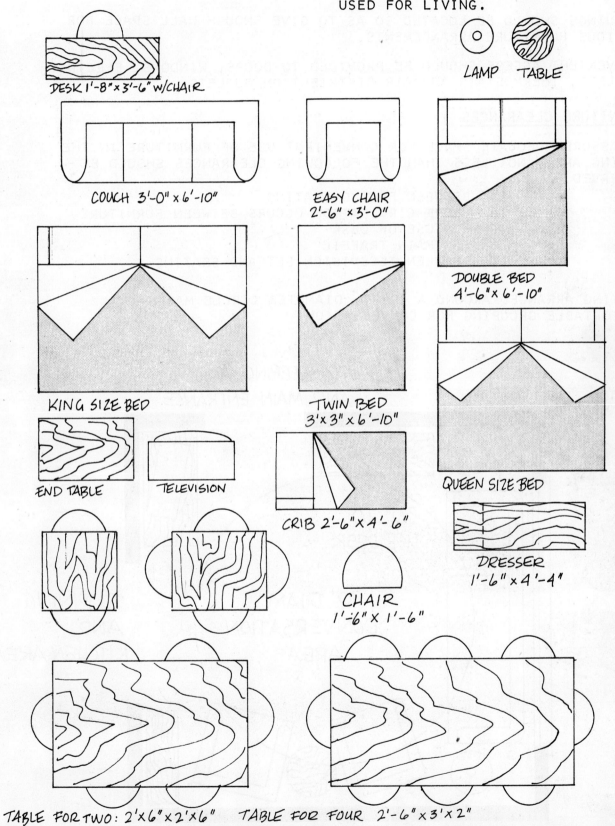

LAMP   TABLE

DESK 1'-8" x 3'-6" w/CHAIR

COUCH 3'-0" x 6'-10"

EASY CHAIR
2'-6" x 3'-0"

DOUBLE BED
4'-6" x 6'-10"

KING SIZE BED

TWIN BED
3' x 3" x 6'-10"

QUEEN SIZE BED

END TABLE   TELEVISION

CRIB 2'-6" x 4'-6"

DRESSER
1'-6" x 4'-4"

CHAIR
1'-6" x 1'-6"

TABLE FOR TWO: 2' x 6" x 2' x 6"   TABLE FOR FOUR 2'-6" x 3' x 2"
DINING TABLE WITH CHAIRS FOR SIX: 3'-4" x 4'-0"; FOR EIGHT: 3'-4" x 6'-0" or
4'-0" x 4'-0"

LIVING AREA

PLANNING CONSIDERATIONS

THRU TRAFFIC SHOULD BE SEPARATED FROM ACTIVITY CENTERS.

OPENINGS SHOULD BE LOCATED SO AS TO GIVE ENOUGH WALL SPACE FOR VARIOUS FURNITURE ARRANGEMENTS.

CONVENIENT ACCESS SHOULD BE PROVIDED TO DOORS, WINDOWS, ELECTRIC OUTLETS, THERMOSTATS AND AIR DISTRIBUTION OUTLETS.

FURNITURE CLEARANCES

TO ASSURE ADEQUATE SPACE FOR CONVENIENT USE OF FURNITURE IN THE LIVING AREA, NOT LESS THAN THE FOLLOWING CLEARANCES SHOULD BE OBSERVED.

        60" BETWEEN FACING SEATING
        24" WHERE CIRCULATION OCCURS BETWEEN FURNITURE
        30" FOR USE OF DESK
        36" FOR MAIN TRAFFIC
        60" BETWEEN TELEVISION SET AND SEATING

SEATING ARRANGED AROUND A 10 FT. DIAMETER CIRCLE MAKES A COMFORTABLE GROUPING FOR CONVERSATION

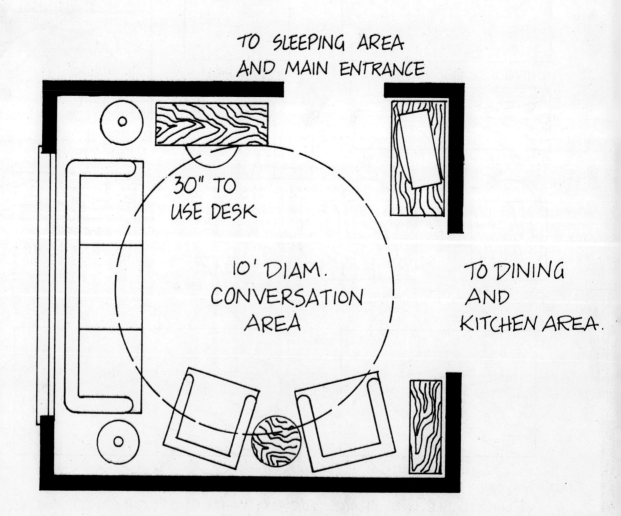

TO SLEEPING AREA AND MAIN ENTRANCE

30" TO USE DESK

10' DIAM. CONVERSATION AREA

TO DINING AND KITCHEN AREA.

DINING AREA

FURNITURE CLEARANCES

TO ASSURE ADEQUATE SPACE FOR CONVENIENT USE OF THE DINING AREA, NOT LESS THAN THE FOLLOWING CLEARANCES FROM THE EDGE OF THE DINING TABLE SHOULD BE OBSERVED.

32" FOR CHAIRS PLUS ACCESS THERETO
38" FOR CHAIRS PLUS ACCESS AND PASSAGE
42" FOR SERVING FROM BEHIND CHAIR
24" FOR PASSAGE ONLY
48" FROM TABLE TO BASE CABINET (IN DINING-KITCHEN)

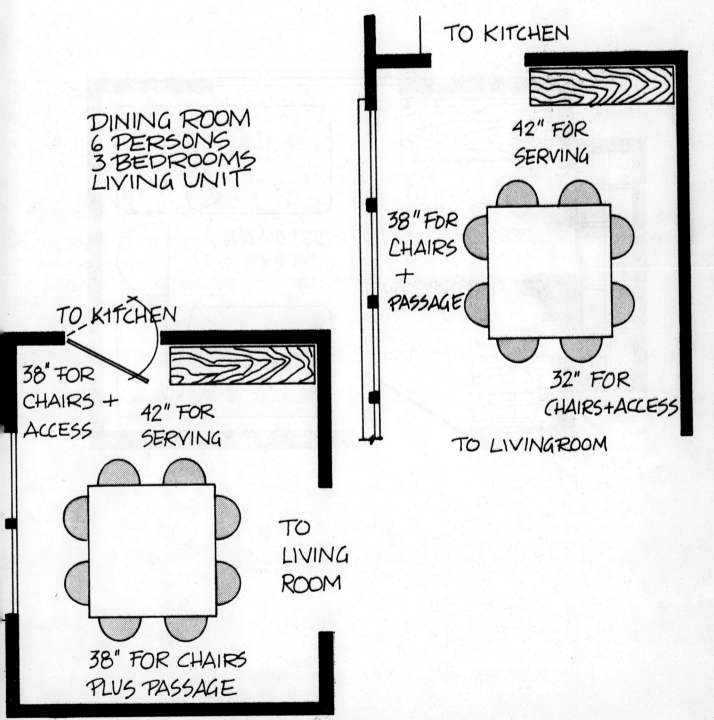

TO KITCHEN

DINING ROOM
6 PERSONS
3 BEDROOMS
LIVING UNIT

42" FOR SERVING

38" FOR CHAIRS + PASSAGE

32" FOR CHAIRS+ACCESS

TO LIVINGROOM

TO KITCHEN

38" FOR CHAIRS + ACCESS

42" FOR SERVING

TO LIVING ROOM

38" FOR CHAIRS PLUS PASSAGE

BEDROOMS

FURNITURE CLEARANCES

TO ASSURE ADEQUATE SPACE FOR CONVENIENT USE OF FURNITURE IN THE
BEDROOM, NOT LESS THAN THE FOLLOWING CLEARANCES SHOULD BE OBSERVED.

42" AT ONE SIDE OR FOOT OF BED FOR DRESSING
12" BETWEEN SIDE OF BED AND SIDE OF DRESSER OR CHEST
36" IN FRONT OF DRESSER, CLOSET AND CHEST OF DRAWERS
24" FOR MAJOR CIRCULATION PATH (DOOR TO CLOSET, ETC.)
22" ON ONE SIDE OF BED FOR CIRCULATION
12" MINIMUM ON LEAST USED SIDE OF BEDS

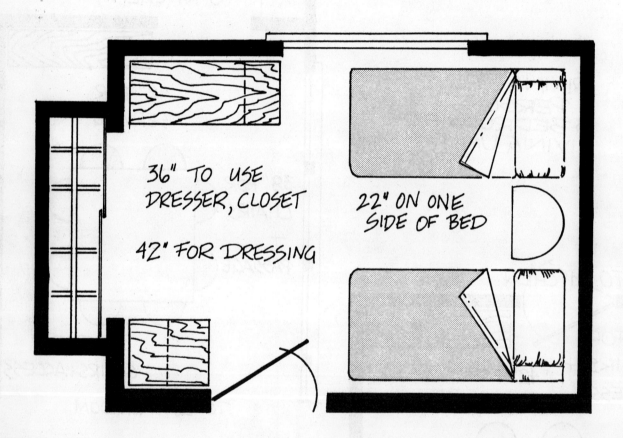

36" TO USE DRESSER, CLOSET

42" FOR DRESSING

22" ON ONE SIDE OF BED

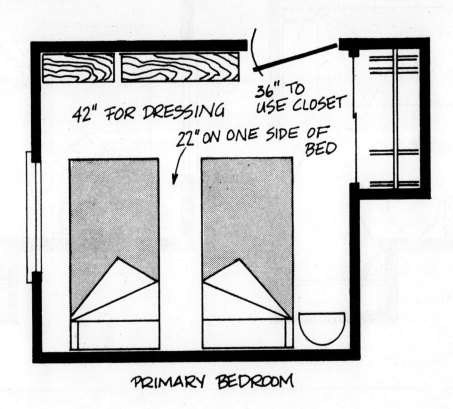

42" FOR DRESSING

36" TO USE CLOSET

22" ON ONE SIDE OF BED

PRIMARY BEDROOM

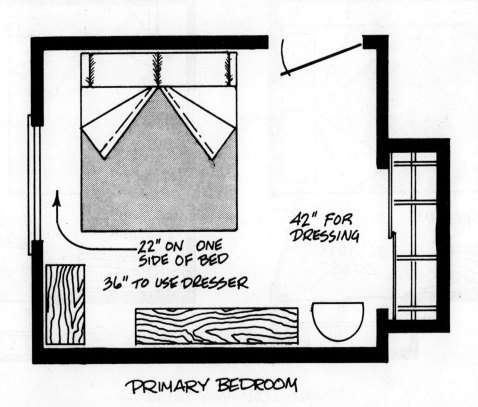

22" ON ONE SIDE OF BED

36" TO USE DRESSER

42" FOR DRESSING

PRIMARY BEDROOM

THE LOCATION OF DOORS AND WINDOWS SHOULD PERMIT ALTERNATE FURNITURE ARRANGEMENTS.

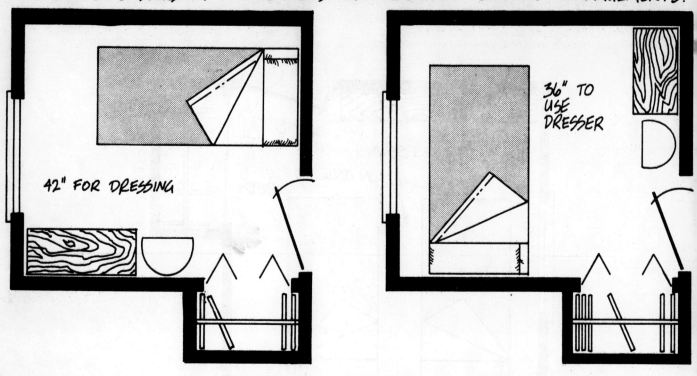

SINGLE OCCUPANCY BEDROOM

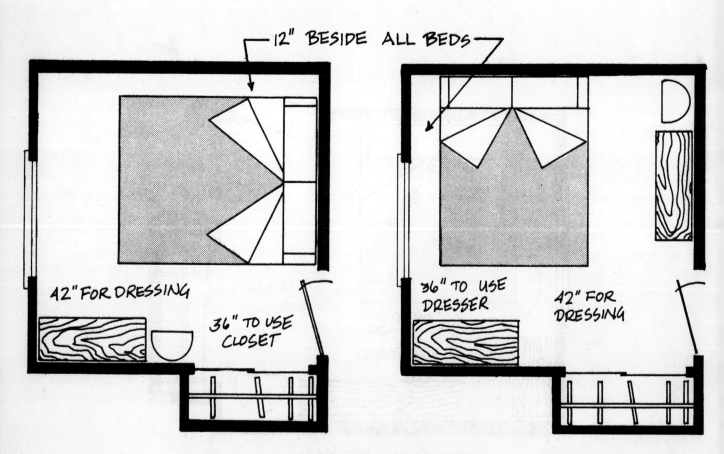

DOUBLE OCCUPANCY BEDROOM

CABINET

RANGE HOOD

30" CLEARANCE
TO BOTTOM OF
UNPROTECTED WOOD
OR METAL CABINET.
MAY BE REDUCED TO
24" WHERE PROTECTION
IS PROVIDED.

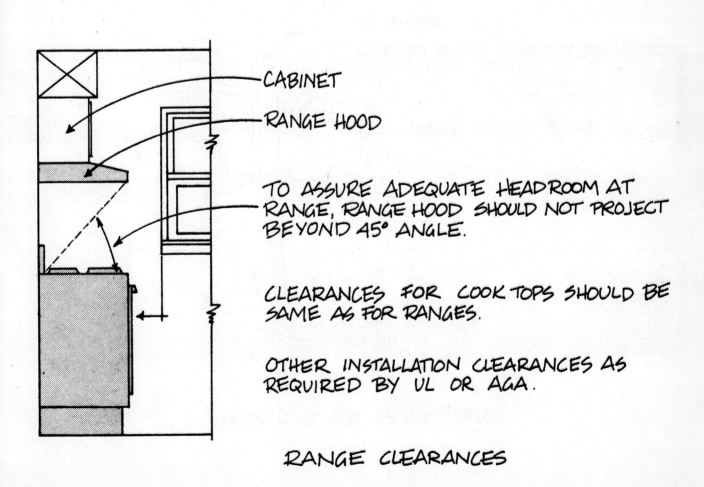

CABINET

RANGE HOOD

TO ASSURE ADEQUATE HEADROOM AT
RANGE, RANGE HOOD SHOULD NOT PROJECT
BEYOND 45° ANGLE.

CLEARANCES FOR COOK TOPS SHOULD BE
SAME AS FOR RANGES.

OTHER INSTALLATION CLEARANCES AS
REQUIRED BY UL OR AGA.

RANGE CLEARANCES

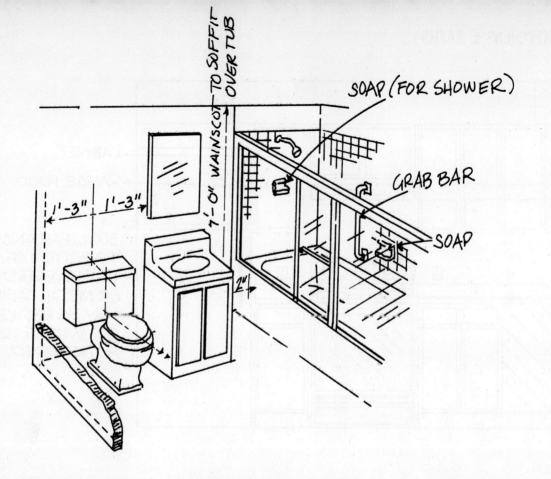

SOAP (FOR SHOWER)

GRAB BAR

SOAP

1'-3" 1'-3"

1'-0" WAINSCOT TO SOFFIT OVER TUB

2"

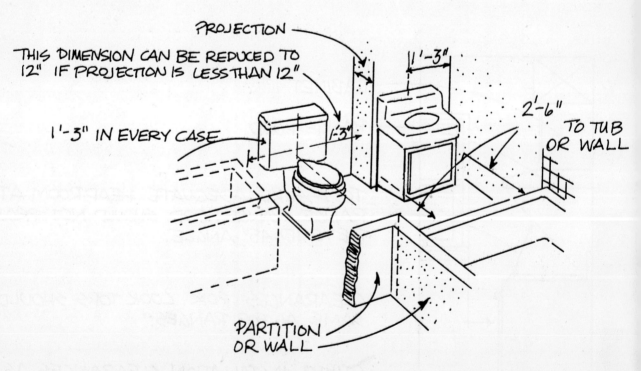

PROJECTION

THIS DIMENSION CAN BE REDUCED TO 12" IF PROJECTION IS LESS THAN 12"

1'-3" IN EVERY CASE

1'-3"

1'-3"

2'-6" TO TUB OR WALL

PARTITION OR WALL

CLEARANCES FOR BATHROOMS

CLOSETS AND STAIRWAYS

CLOTHES RODS SHOULD BE MOUNTED AT LEAST 5' CLEAR OF FLOOR OR
OBSTRUCTIONS - BUT NOT MORE THAN 6'8" ABOVE FLOOR.

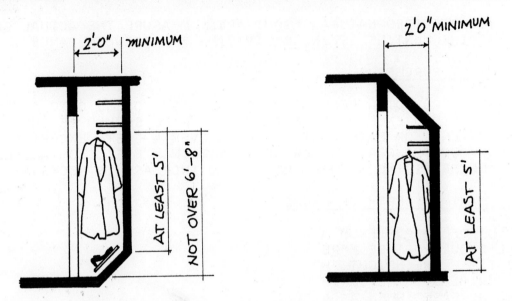

USE OF SLIP RESISTANT TREADS IS RECOMMENDED.

USE OF OPEN RISERS IS DISCOURAGED (THEIR USE IS NOT PERMITTED IN
HOUSING FOR THE ELDERLY AND HANDICAPPED AND IN CARE-TYPE HOUSING).

USE OF OVERLY LARGE, TOE-CATCHING NOSINGS IS DISCOURAGED IN HOUSING
FOR THE ELDERLY AND HANDICAPPED.

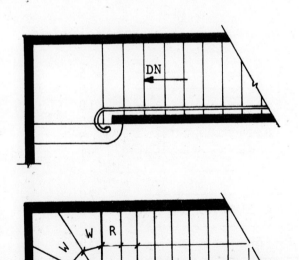

FLIGHT OF TWO RISERS
PUBLIC OR PRIVATE STAIRS

WINDERS, PRIVATE STAIRS

W cannot be less than
R for typical run

LIGHTING

NATURAL LIGHTING

MEASURE OF WINDOW LIGHT AREA

IN DETERMINING REQUIRED NATURAL LIGHT AREA, MEASURE THE ACTUAL GLASS AREA DISREGARDING MUNTINS (SLENDER DIVIDING BAR BETWEEN PANES).

NATURAL LIGHT AT PORCHES

WHEN AN OPENING PROVIDING REQUIRED NATURAL LIGHT OPENS ONTO A COVERED PORCH WHOSE DEPTH EXCEEDS 4 FEET, THE OPENING SHOULD BE INCREASED IN AREA 10 PERCENT FOR EACH FOOT OF DEPTH OVER 4 FEET, EXCEPT IF THE SIDE OF THE PROJECTED PORCH COVERING IS WITHIN 4 FEET FROM ANY EDGE OF THE OPENING PROVIDING NATURAL LIGHT, NO INCREASE IS NECESSARY.

RECOMMENDED MAXIMUM DEPTH OF ROOMS

THE DEPTH "D' OF A ROOM FROM A WINDOW WALL SHOULD NOT BE MORE THAN 2-1/2 TIMES THE HEIGHT "H" OF THE WINDOW HEAD. THE DEPTH "D" MAY BE INCREASED WHEN A SIDE WINDOW IS PROVIDED OR WHEN MORE THAN THE MINIMUM AMOUNT OF NATURAL LIGHT IS PROVIDED.

RECOMMENDED MINIMUM ILLUMINATION FOR DWELLINGS

THE FOLLOWING TABLE SHOWS LEVELS OF ILLUMINATION FOR SAFETY IN AND AROUND THE DWELLING.

LOCATION	FOOTCANDLES
GENERAL LIGHTING	
FOR SAFETY IN PASSAGE AREA - HALLS	5
STAIRS	10
AREAS PRIMARILY FOR RELAXATION	10
AREAS INVOLVING VISUAL TASK	30
ENTRANCES AND EXTERIOR STEPS	5
EXTERIOR WALKWAY SURFACE	1
SPECIFIC VISUAL TASKS	
KITCHEN ACTIVITIES: SINK	70
RANGE AND WORK SURFACES	50
LAUNDRY ACTIVITIES: IRONING	50
WASHER AND DRYER	30
BATHROOM AT THE MIRROR	50

ARTIFICIAL LIGHTING

STAIR LIGHTING

STAIRS RANK HIGH AS CAUSES OF ACCIDENTS IN DWELLINGS. ONE WAY TO
REDUCE THE NUMBER OF ACCIDENTS IS TO HAVE ADEQUATE LIGHT THAT DOES
NOT CAST SHADOWS UPON THE TREADS.

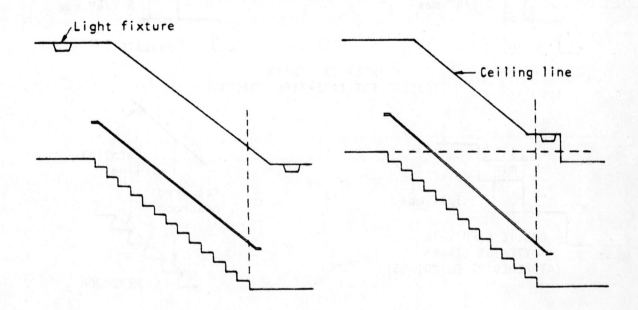

TO ACCOMPLISH THIS, PROVIDE A LIGHT FIXTURE AT BOTH THE TOP AND THE
BOTTOM OF STAIRS AND USE A LIGHT-REFLECTING COLOR ON THE CEILING.
THE BOTTOM LIGHT FIXTURE SHOULD BE BEYOND THE LOWEST RISER.

ONE FIXTURE IS ADEQUATE WHEN LOCATED HIGHER THAN THE TOP RISER AND
BEYOND THE BOTTOM RISER. THIS LOCATION PRODUCES A SHADOW OF A
PERSON ASCENDING THE STAIRS. HOWEVER, THIS IS THE LESS HAZARDOUS
DIRECTION OF TRAVEL. A SOFT DIFFUSED LIGHT SHOULD BE USED TO PRE-
VENT A GLARE THAT MIGHT BLIND A PERSON DESCENDING THE STAIRS.

HANDRAILS AND RAILINGS

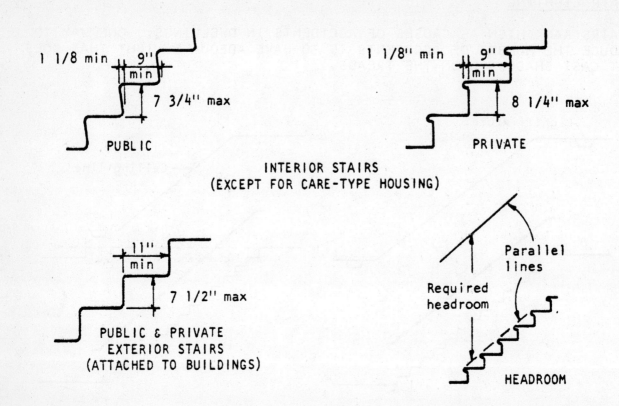

1 1/8 min   9" min   7 3/4" max
PUBLIC

1 1/8" min   9" min   8 1/4" max
PRIVATE

INTERIOR STAIRS
(EXCEPT FOR CARE-TYPE HOUSING)

11" min   7 1/2" max

PUBLIC & PRIVATE
EXTERIOR STAIRS
(ATTACHED TO BUILDINGS)

Parallel lines
Required headroom
HEADROOM

HANDRAIL AND RAILING DETAILS

HANDRAILS SHOULD BE PLACED ON THE RIGHT SIDE OF STAIRS, DESCENDING.
HORIZONTAL DIMENSION OF HANDRAIL (GRIP) SHOULD NOT EXCEED 2-5/8".
HANDRAILS SHOULD RETURN TO WALL OR FLOOR, OR TERMINATE IN A POST,
SCROLL OR LOOP (MANDATORY FOR HOUSING FOR ELDERLY OR HANDICAPPED).
MOUNTING HEIGHT FOR STAIR HANDRAILS SHOULD BE 30" TO 34". RAILING
HEIGHT FOR STOOPS, PORCHES, ETC. SHOULD BE AT LEAST 30"
(42" MANDATORY FOR EXTERIOR CORRIDORS, BALCONIES, ROOF DECKS).

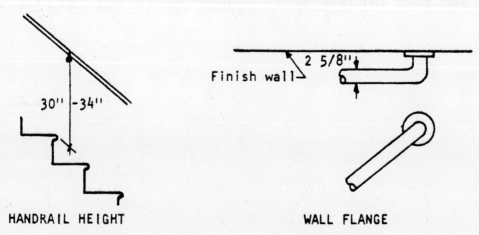

30" -34"

HANDRAIL HEIGHT

Finish wall   2 5/8"

WALL FLANGE

VENTILATION

ATTIC VENTS ENTIRELY IN EAVE OR ENTIRELY
NEAR THE RIDGE ARE ACCEPTABLE MEANS OF
VENTILATION. HOWEVER, A COMBINATION OF
EAVE AND RIDGE VENTILATION IS DESIRABLE
TO PROVIDE A THERMAL HEAD TO INDUCE
AIR FLOW.

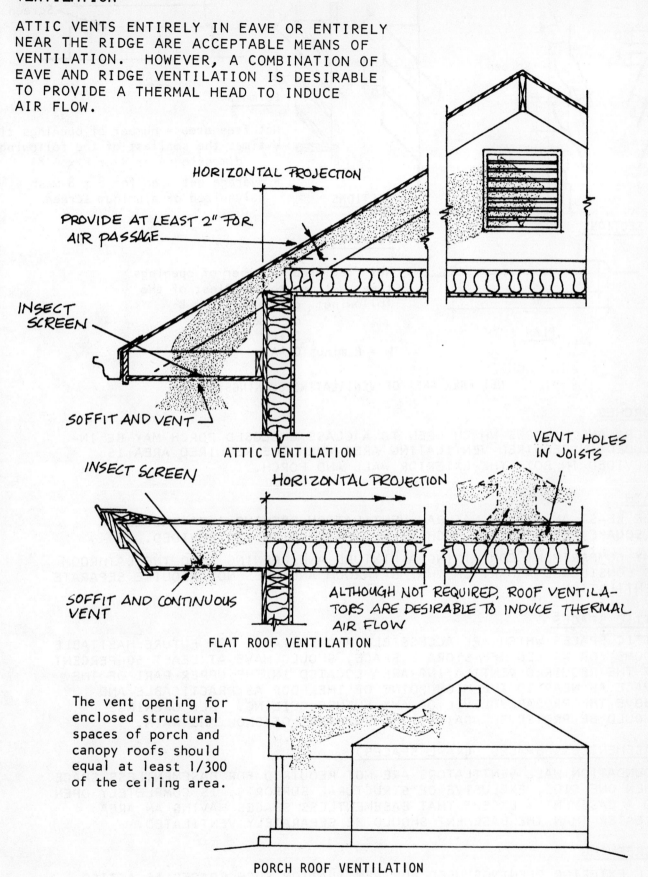

HORIZONTAL PROJECTION

PROVIDE AT LEAST 2" FOR
AIR PASSAGE

INSECT
SCREEN

SOFFIT AND VENT

ATTIC VENTILATION

INSECT SCREEN

HORIZONTAL PROJECTION

VENT HOLES
IN JOISTS

SOFFIT AND CONTINUOUS
VENT

ALTHOUGH NOT REQUIRED, ROOF VENTILA-
TORS ARE DESIRABLE TO INDUCE THERMAL
AIR FLOW

FLAT ROOF VENTILATION

The vent opening for
enclosed structural
spaces of porch and
canopy roofs should
equal at least 1/300
of the ceiling area.

PORCH ROOF VENTILATION

21

VENTILATION (CONTINUED)

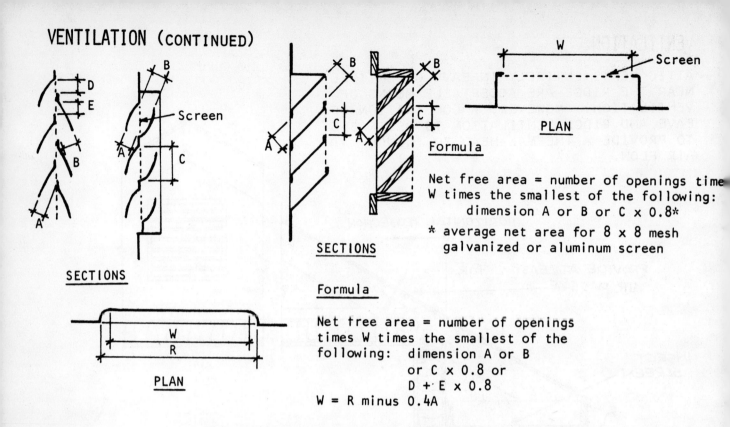

SECTIONS

PLAN

Formula

Net free area = number of openings time
W times the smallest of the following:
dimension A or B or C x 0.8*

* average net area for 8 x 8 mesh
galvanized or aluminum screen

SECTIONS

Formula

Net free area = number of openings
times W times the smallest of the
following: dimension A or B
or C x 0.8 or
D + E x 0.8
W = R minus 0.4A

NET FREE AREA OF VENTILATING OPENINGS

PORCHES

DOORS AND WINDOWS WHICH OPEN TO A GLASS ENCLOSED PORCH MAY BE IN-
CLUDED IN REQUIRED VENTILATING AREA WHEN THE REQUIRED AREA IS
PROVIDED IN BOTH THE EXTERIOR WALL AND PORCH.

BATH

THE LEAST AMOUNT OF NATURAL VENTILATION OPENING AREA SHOULD BE
3 SQUARE FEET, UNLESS MECHANICAL VENTILATION IS PROVIDED.

ANY COMPARTMENT CONTAINING A FIXTURE AND OPENING INTO THE BATHROOM
IS CONSIDERED A PART OF THAT BATHROOM AND DOES NOT REQUIRE SEPARATE
VENTILATION.

ATTIC SPACES

ATTIC SPACES WHICH ARE ACCESSIBLE AND SUITABLE FOR FUTURE HABITABLE
ROOMS, OR WALLED-OFF STORAGE SPACE, SHOULD HAVE AT LEAST 50 PERCENT
OF THE REQUIRED VENTILATING AREA LOCATED IN THE UPPER PART OF THE
SPACE AS NEAR TO THE HIGH POINT OF THE ROOF AS PRACTICABLE AND
ABOVE THE PROBABLE LEVEL OF ANY FUTURE CEILING. ALL OPENINGS
SHOULD BE PROTECTED AGAINST THE ENTRANCE OF SNOW AND RAIN.

BASEMENTLESS SPACES (CRAWL SPACES)

FOUNDATION WALL VENTILATORS ARE NOT REQUIRED FOR BASEMENTLESS SPACE
WHEN ONE SIDE, EXCLUSIVE OF STRUCTURAL SUPPORTS, IS COMPLETELY OPEN
TO A BASEMENT - EXCEPT THAT BASEMENTLESS SPACES HAVING AN AREA
GREATER THAN THE BASEMENT SHOULD BE SEPARATELY VENTILATED.

SCREENING

ALL EXTERIOR OPENINGS USED FOR VENTILATION SUCH SPACES AS ATTICS
AND CRAWL SPACES SHOULD BE SCREENED WITH AT LEAST 8 MESH PER INCH
SCREENING.

INTRODUCTION TO CHOOSING YOUR PLANS

Now that we have given you pertinent information about: furniture dimensions and placement; kitchens; baths; closets; stairways; lighting; handrails; and ventilation —let's go back.

In choosing a house plan, it is most important that you have enough room for your needs now and in the future. But too much room can be just as inconvenient (and much more costly) than not enough. If you are planning a family, it is wise to provide for childrens' bedrooms rather than be faced with moving or adding on extra rooms at a later date. If your family is growing, and they do grow fast, take into consideration not only what you need now but what you are going to need in the future. And when your family is grown, think of what rooms can be smaller or eliminated.

Are you thinking that you will never build more than one house? You are part of a transient population. Today, you can be residing in the east only to be told next month that your employer is moving his operation to the west coast or down south. This means a new home! Perhaps there is a job opportunity that just can't be turned down—in a location beyond feasible commuting distance—this means a new home! It is also the time to re-evaluate your needs. Is your family growing in number, growing in size, or has it decreased? Does anyone in the family suffer from a physical handicap? Do you own antiques with which you do not wish to part? Do you have a library of books too valuable to dispose of, or a collection of anything which you want to display? Do you work (carry on a business) at home? The answers to these questions should help you choose a home plan which exactly meets your needs.

Again: if your family is young, remember a child will grow into the need of privacy. Choose a plan with a bedroom large enough to take care of his future needs—an easy chair, larger desk, stereo equipment, space for working on hobbies, etc. If the family is growing, make sure there is a place for the young adult's entertainment which will not interfere with the rest of the household. If the family is smaller in number, you could cut down on the number of bedrooms. If there is a physically handicapped person, give careful consideration to a ranch type home. If you prefer a split level or traditional two story home, make sure there are all the necessary facilities on one floor for his convenience. If you have valued antiques, furniture in particular, look carefully at room measurements and lay-outs to give these cherished possessions the setting due them. (The editor purchased her latest home with one requirement—a dining room which would accommodate her antique dining room set). If you have a library or a collection you wish to display, choose a plan with a room suitable for this purpose. Likewise, if you have need for an office, many times an extra bedroom can be converted for that use, without time, trouble, or expense.

And all this brings to mind—to make sure you have the space you need, and want —get a supply of graph paper of ¼" spaces. Take the dimensions of the rooms in the home plan (or plans) which interests you most and using the graph paper with a scale of ¼" equalling 1 foot, make a diagram of each room. Now, you play a child's game with an adult's purpose! With the measurements given on pages 8 and 9, or using your own actual measurements, make layouts of the various rooms with the furniture you have. Are there alternate layouts, or must the furniture forever stay in one place? The best liked plans are worthless if the furniture is too crowded for comfortable usage. By the same token, if you have fine quality furniture (but not many pieces) and do not want to buy more, it isn't a practical idea to buy plans for a home with extra large rooms. This would only emphasize the lack of furniture and the pieces would lose their effectiveness and beauty. Be realistic in this respect for if you are not comfortable in your home, you will grow to dislike it—even if you live in it for only a minimal length of time, it will seem at least twice that long.

Choosing a home plan takes consideration. You must not pick one on impulse. Mentally, walk through it. Envision each room as you would like it. Imagine a typical day in the house. Think about its convenience for cooking, cleaning, laundry, entertaining, relaxing. Remember it's not like buying a pair of shoes on impulse and never wearing them. You can throw them away without much conscience—but who can afford to discard an unsuitable, uncomfortable house in the same manner!

Building a home can be fun, pleasurable and satisfactory—and it should be. If you do your homework in careful planning, sensible thinking, always with patience and determination, you'll be a happy homeowner.

The Unique Beauty of English Tudor

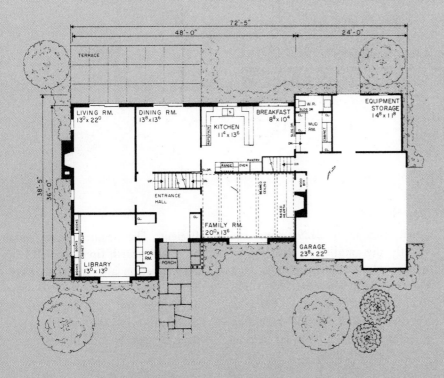

Design S 2148

1,656 Sq. Ft. — First Floor
1,565 Sq. Ft. — Second Floor
48,292 Cu. Ft.

The charm of this Tudor adaptation could hardly be improved upon. Its fine proportion and exquisite use of materials result in a most distinctive home. However, the tremendous exterior appeal tells only half of the story. Inside there is a breathtaking array of highlights which will cater to the whims of the large family. Imagine six large bedrooms, two full baths and plenty of closets on the second floor! The first floor has a formal living zone made up of the big living room, the separate dining room, and the sizeable library. A second zone is comprised of the U-shaped kitchen, the breakfast room, and the family room - all contributing to fine informal family living patterns. Behind the garage is the mud room, wash room, and the practical equipment storage room. Don't miss beamed ceiling, powder room, two fireplaces, and two flights of stairs to the basement.

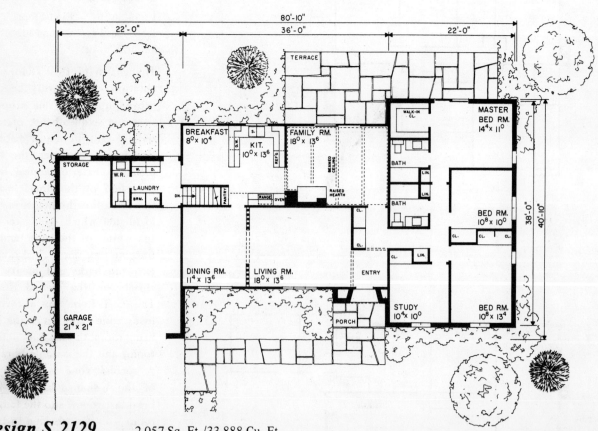

Design S 2129   2,057 Sq. Ft./33,888 Cu. Ft.

Here, on these two pages, are a couple of Old English adaptations. Note both the similarities and dissimilarities of their exteriors and their floor plans. The floor plans are essentially the same except that they are planned in reverse of one an-

other. **Design S 2129**, above, is slightly the smaller of the two designs in both square footage and overall length. However, its livability is in no way inferior. The rear kitchen flanked by the breakfast room and cozy family room is most

efficient. The beamed ceiling and the raised hearth fireplace will help create a warm and cheerful atmosphere. Handy to the entrances from the garage and rear yard are the basement stairs. Here will be extra space for storage and hobbies.

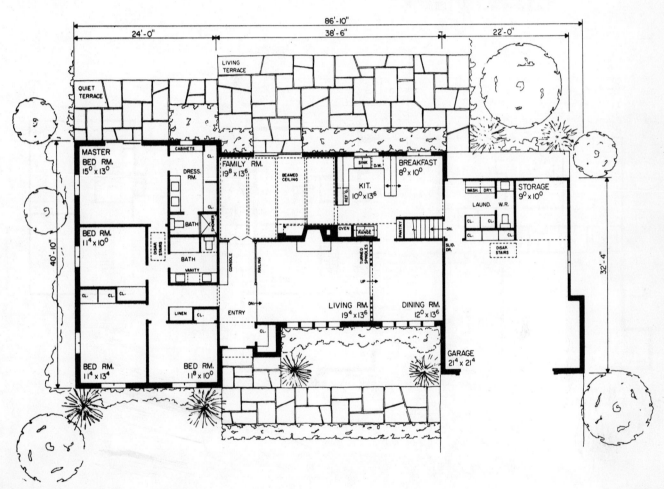

Design S 1989   2,282 Sq. Ft./41,831 Cu. Ft.

This is high style reminiscent of Old England with a plan as contemporary as today and tomorrow. There is, indeed, a feeling of coziness that emanates from the ground-hugging qualities of this picturesque home. Inside, there is livability galore.

There's the four bedroom, two bath sleeping wing with a dressing room as a bonus. There's the sunken living room and the separate dining room to function as the family's formal living area. Then, overlooking the rear yard, there's the infor-

mal living area with its beamed ceiling family room and wonderful kitchen with its adjacent breakfast room. As a positive plus to outstanding livability, there's the handy first floor laundry with its wash room. Don't miss the storage room.

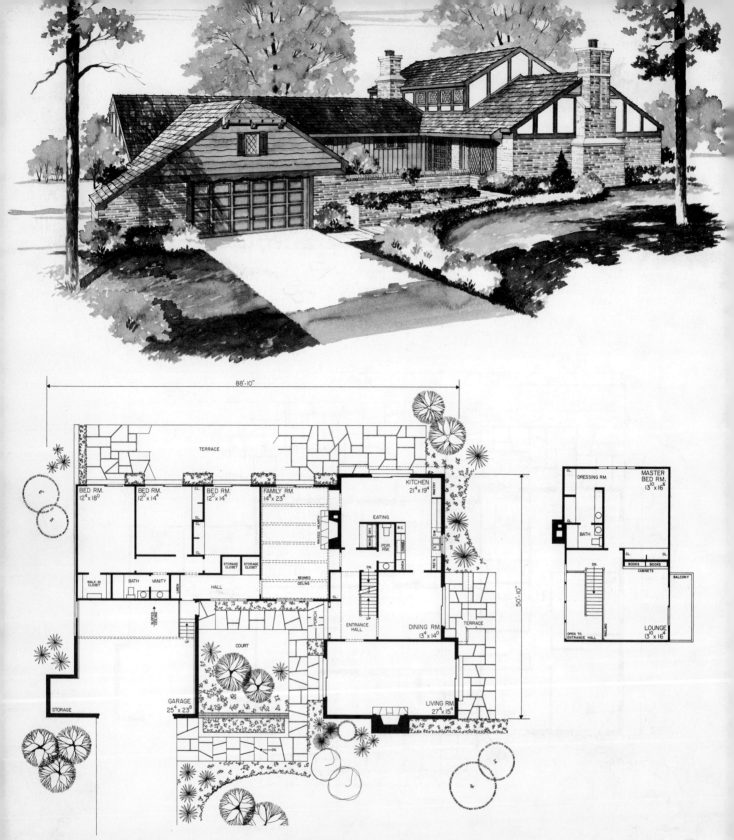

Design S 2373
2,634 Sq. Ft.-First Floor/819 Sq. Ft.-Second Floor/47,867 Cu. Ft.

What a wonderfully different and imposing two-story design this is! The Tudor styling and the varying roof planes, along with its U-shape, add to the air of distinction. From the driveway, steps lead past a big raised planter up to the enclosed entrance court. A wide overhanging roof shelters the massive patterned double doors flanked by diamond paned side lites. The living room is outstanding. It is located a distance from other living areas and is quite spacious. The centered fireplace is the dominant feature, while sliding glass doors open from each end onto outdoor terraces. The kitchen, too, is spacious and functions well. Two eating areas are nearby. It is worth noting that each of the major first floor rooms have direct access to the outdoor terraces. Note second floor suite.

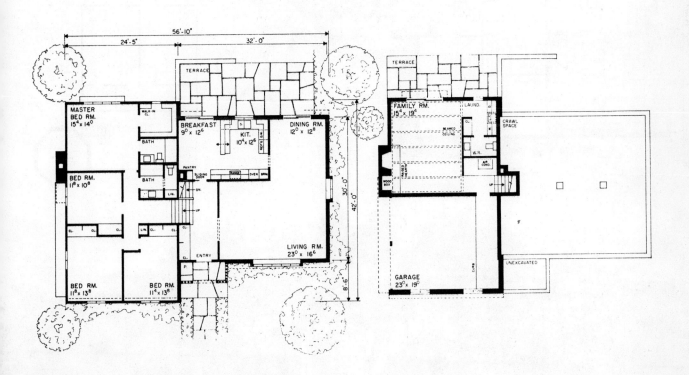

Design S 2137   987 Sq. Ft.—Main Level/1,043 Sq. Ft.—Upper Level/463 Sq. Ft. Lower Level/29,382 Cu. Ft.

Tudor design adapts to split level living. The result is an unique charm for all to remember. As for the livability, the happy occupants of this tri-level home will experience wonderful living patterns. A covered porch protects, and adds charm to the front entry. The center hall routes traffic conveniently to the spacious formal living and dining area; the informal breakfast room and kitchen zone; the upper level bedrooms; the lower level all-purpose family room. Contributing to fine living are such highlights as 2 1/2 baths, walk-in closet, four bedrooms, sliding glass doors, pass-thru from kitchen to breakfast room, beamed ceiling, raised hearth fireplace, separate laundry, and an attached two-car garage. Note the two terraces.

Design S 2391

2,496 Sq. Ft.-First Floor/958 Sq. Ft.-Second Floor/59,461 Cu. Ft.

Here is a stately English adaptation that is impressive, indeed. The two-story octagonal foyer strikes a delightfully authentic design note. The entrance hall with open staircase and two-story ceiling is spacious. Clustered around the efficient kitchen are the formal living areas and those catering to informal activites. The family room with its beamed ceiling and raised hearth fireplace functions, like the formal living/dining zone, with the partially enclosed outdoor terrace. Three bedrooms with two baths comprise the first floor sleeping zone. Each room will enjoy its access to the terrace. Upstairs there are two more bedrooms and a study. Notice the sliding glass doors to the balcony and how the study looks down into the entrance hall. The three-car garage is great!

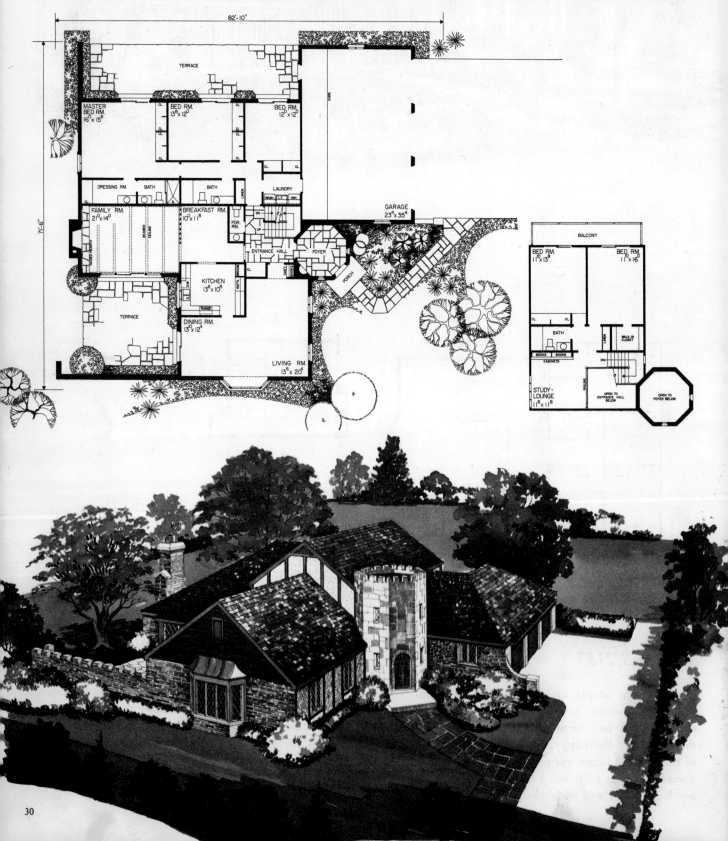

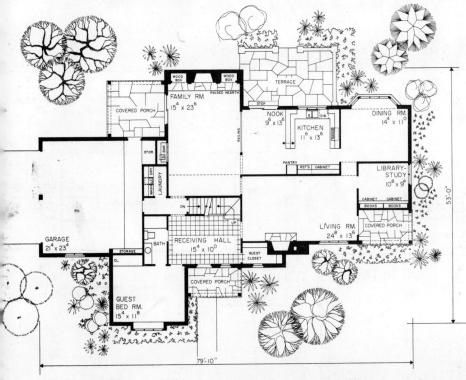

Design S 2356

1,969 Sq. Ft. — First Floor
1,702 Sq. Ft. — Second Floor
55,105 Cu. Ft.

Here is truly an exquisite Tudor adaptation. The exterior, with its interesting roof lines, its window treatment, its stately chimney, and its appealing use of brick and stucco, could hardly be more dramatic. Inside, the drama really begins to unfold as one envisions his family's living patterns. The delightfully large receiving hall has a two story ceiling and controls the flexible traffic patterns. The living and dining rooms, with the library nearby, will cater to the formal living pursuits. The guest room offers another haven for the enjoyment of peace and quiet. Observe the adjacent full bath. Just inside the entrance from the garage is the laundry room. For the family's informal living activities there are the interactions of the family room - covered porch - nook - kitchen zone. Notice the raised hearth fireplace, the wood boxes, the sliding glass doors, built-in bar, and the kitchen passthru. Adding to the charm of the family room is its high ceiling. From the second floor hall one can look down and observe the activities below.

Design S 2605

1,775 Sq. Ft./34,738 Cu. Ft.

Here are three modified L-shaped Tudor designs with tremendous exterior appeal and fine efficient floor plans. While each plan features three bedrooms and 2½ baths, the square footage differences are interesting. Note that each design may be built with or without a basement. This appealing exterior is highlighted by a variety of roof planes, patterned brick, wavy-edged siding, and a massive chimney. The garage is oversized and has good storage potential. In addition to the entrance court, there are two covered porches and two terraces for outdoor living.

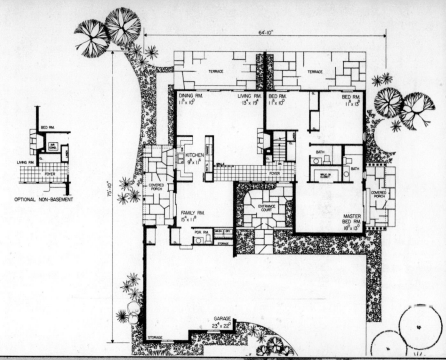

Design S 2606

1,499 Sq. Ft./29,266 Cu. Ft.

This modest sized house with its 1,499 square feet could hardly offer more in the way of exterior charm and interior livability. Measuring only 60 feet in width means it will not require a huge, expensive piece of property. The orientation of the garage and the front drive court are features which promote an economical use of property. In addition to the formal, separate living and dining rooms, there are the informal kitchen-family room areas. Note the beamed ceiling, the fireplace, the sliding glass doors, and the eating area of the family room.

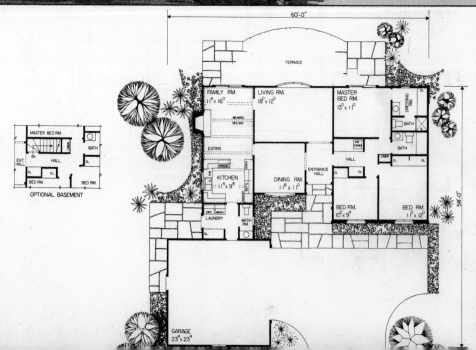

Design S 2604

1,956 Sq. Ft./44,950 Cu. Ft.

A feature that will set the whole wonderful pattern of true family living will be the 26 foot wide country kitchen. The spacious, L-shaped kitchen has its efficiency enhanced by the island counter work surface. Beamed ceilings, fireplace, and sliding glass doors add to the cozy atmosphere of this area. The laundry, dining room, and entry hall are but a step or two away. The big keeping room also has a fireplace and can function with the terrace, also. Observe the 2½ baths.

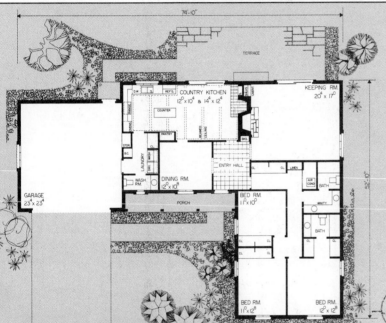

OPTIONAL BASEMENT

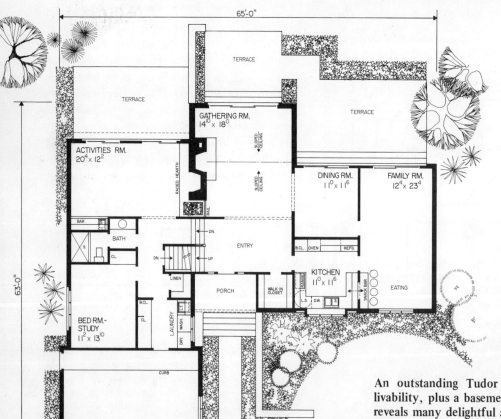

Design S 2758

1,143 Sq. Ft. — Main Level
770 Sq. Ft. — Lower Level
792 Sq. Ft. — Upper Level
43,085 Cu. Ft.

An outstanding Tudor with three levels of exceptional livability, plus a basement. A careful study of the exterior reveals many delightful architectural details which give this home a character of its own. Notice the appealing recessed front entrance. Observe the overhanging roof with the exposed rafters. Don't miss the window treatment, the use of stucco and simulated beams, the masses of brick and the stylish chimney. Inside, the living potential is unsurpassed. Imagine, there are three living areas - the gathering, family and activities rooms. With the snack bar, informal eating area and dining room, eating patterns can be flexible. In addition to the three bedroom, two-bath upper level, there is a fourth bedroom with adjacent bath on the lower level. Then there is the laundry, fireplaces, etc., etc.

77'-8"

48'-8"

LEDGE
TUB
BATH
MASTER BED RM.
17⁰ x 13⁶
DRSG. RM.
VANITY
WALK-IN CLOSET
WALK-IN CLOSET
BATH
LINEN
TWLS
CL.
CL.

DINING RM.
12⁸ x 11⁶

REF.
S
D.W.
KITCHEN
13⁴ x 11⁶
SNACK BAR

FAMILY RM.
15⁴ x 15⁶
WASH RM.

SERVICE ENT.
CL.

BRM CL.
OVEN
RANGE
PANTRY

DN
OPEN TO PLANTER BELOW
RAILING
UP
SLOPED CEILING
ENTRANCE
LEDGE

LIVING RM.
20⁰ x 13⁰

CURB

GARAGE
22⁸ x 21⁶
STOR.

CL.
PDR. RM.
PORCH

BED RM.
11⁶ x 13⁰

STUDY
9² x 13⁰

TERRACE

TERRACE

ACTIVITIES RM.
22⁸ x 15⁶

BSM'T.

CRAWL

BATH
CL.
CL.
UP
DN

UNEX.

UNEX.

BED RM.
10⁸ x 10⁶

HOBBY & SEWING RM.
11⁶ x 10⁶

2095077

Design S 2773

1,157 Sq. Ft. — Main Level
950 Sq. Ft. — Upper Level
912 Sq. Ft. — Lower Level
44,354 Cu. Ft.

Another Tudor with tri-level livability plus a basement for extra storage potential. This adaptation has an appealing ground-hugging quality. The upper level dramatically overhangs the lower level, while the covered front porch effectively shelters the front entrance, the box-bay muntined window. The delightfully proportioned exterior is complimented by the prudent use of such contrasting materials as stucco, brick, stone and simulated wood beams. The large, active family will find its many pursuits more than adequately housed. Imagine, a formal living room, plus an all-purpose activities room. If necessary, this home could provide five bedrooms. Otherwise, there is the quiet study and the handy hobby and sewing room. As for bath facilities, there are three full baths, a wash room and a powder room. All strategically located. A most pleasing feature will be the open balcony effect of the main and upper levels which look down on the lower level planting area. Then, of course, there is the separate dining room, the snack bar and the two outdoor terraces.

Design S 2278

1,804 Sq. Ft.-First Floor/939 Sq. Ft.-Second Floor/44,274 Cu. Ft.

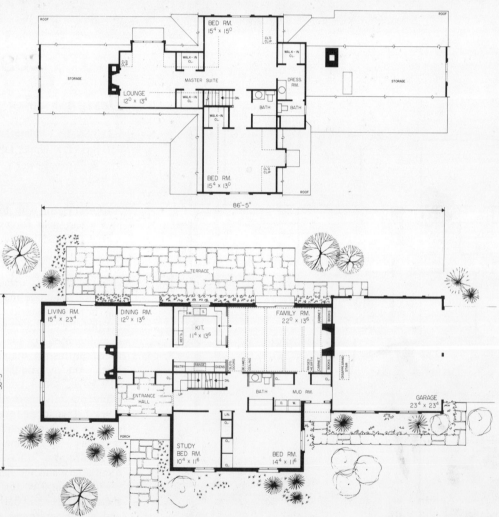

This cozy Tudor adaptation is surely inviting. Its friendly demeanor seems to say, "welcome". Upon admittance to the formal front entrance hall, even the most casual of visitors will be filled with anticipation at the prospect of touring the house. And little wonder, too. Traffic patterns are efficient. Room relationships are excellent. A great feature is the location of the living, dining, kitchen, and family rooms across the back of the house. Each enjoys a view of the rear yard and sliding glass doors provide direct access to the terrace. Another outstanding feature is the flexibility of the sleeping patterns. This may be a five bedroom house, or one with three bedrooms with study and lounge. Don't miss the three fireplaces and three baths.

Design S 2373   1,160 Sq. Ft.-First Floor/1,222 Sq. Ft.-Second Floor/33,775 Cu. Ft.

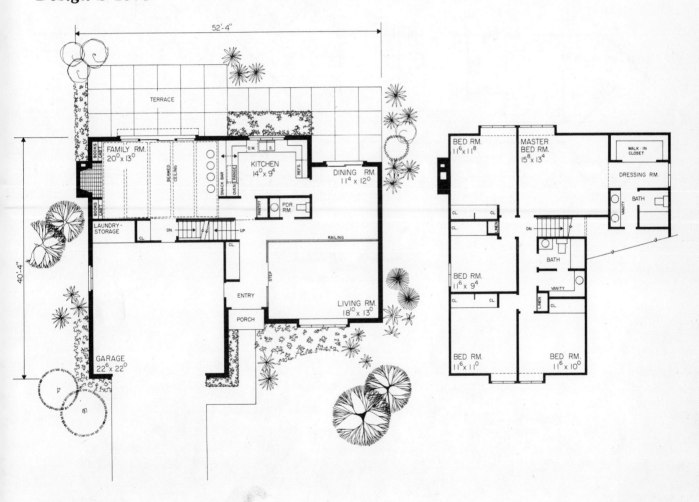

Finding more livability wrapped in such an attractive facade would be difficult, indeed. This charming Tudor adaptation will return big dividends per construction dollar. It is compact and efficient. And, of course, it will not require a big, expensive piece of property. The location of the two-car garage as an integral part of the structure has its convenience and economic advantages, too. The living room is sunken and is divided from the dining room by a railing which helps maintain the desirable spacious atmosphere. The family room with its beamed ceiling, attractive fireplace wall, built-in storage, and snack bar functions well with both the kitchen and the outdoor terrace. Four bedrooms, two baths, plenty of closets, and built-in vanities are among highlights of second floor.

Design S 2317   3,161 Sq. Ft. / 57,900 Cu. Ft.

Here's a rambling English manor with its full measure of individuality. Its fine proportions and irregular shape offer even the most casual of passers-by delightful views of fine architecture. The exterior boasts an interesting use of varying materials. In addition to the brick work, there is vertical siding, wavy-edged horizontal siding and stucco. Three massive chimneys provide each of the three major wings with a fireplace. The overhanging roof provides the cover for the long front porch. Note the access to both the foyer as well as the service hall. The formal living room, with its sloping beamed ceiling, and fireplace flanked by book shelves and cabinets, will be cozy, indeed. Study rest of plan. It's outstanding. Don't miss the three fireplaces and three full baths.

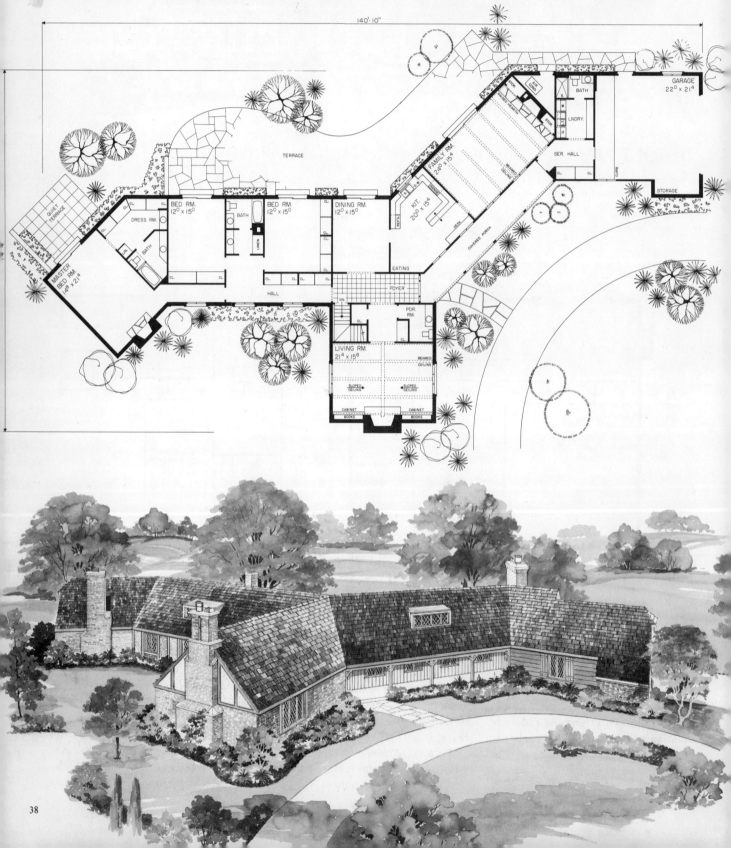

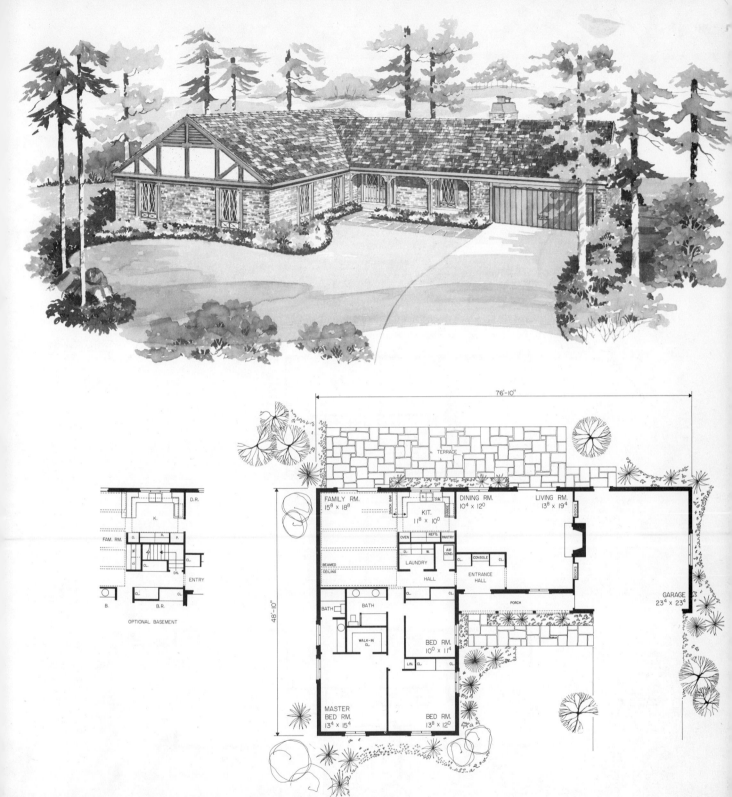

FAMILY RM. 15⁸ x 18⁸

KIT. 11⁸ x 10⁰

DINING RM. 10⁴ x 12⁰

LIVING RM. 13⁸ x 19⁴

TERRACE

BEAMED CEILING

LAUNDRY

HALL

ENTRANCE HALL

PORCH

GARAGE 23⁴ x 23⁴

BATH

BATH

WALK-IN CL.

BED RM. 10⁰ x 11⁴

MASTER BED RM. 13⁴ x 15⁴

BED RM. 13⁸ x 12⁰

76'-10"

48'-10"

OPTIONAL BASEMENT

D.R.

K.

FAM. RM.

ENTRY

B.

B.R.

Design S 2277   1,903 Sq. Ft. / 25,087 Cu. Ft.

Tudor design front and center! And what an impact this beautifully proportioned L-shaped home does deliver. Observe the numerous little design features which make this such an attractive home. The half-timber work, the window styling, the front door detailing, the covered porch post brackets, and the chimney are all among the eye-pleasing highlights. Well zoned, the dining and living rooms are openly planned for formal dining and living. On the opposite side of the kitchen is the informal, multi-purpose family room. There is a snack bar and kitchen pass-thru for those quick breakfasts and lunches. Sliding glass doors permit both living areas to function with the outdoor terrace. The sleeping zone is the projecting wing. It features three bedrooms, two baths.

Design S 2275
1,421 Sq. Ft.-First Floor/1,456 Sq. Ft.-Second Floor/45,330 Cu. Ft.

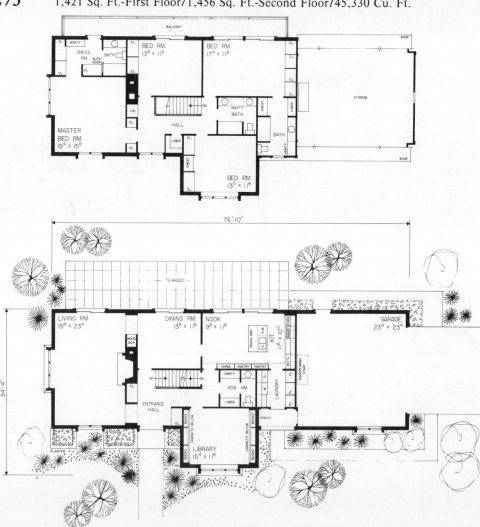

This stately Tudor version is impressive, indeed. The fine proportion and architectural detailing give it a distinctive character all its own. Upon passing through the double front doors one is quickly aware of the excellent traffic circulation. Notice how the entrance hall routes traffic to the various rooms. The end living room will enjoy the utmost in privacy. No unnecessary cross-room traffic here. The dining room is but a step or two from the hallway, the living room and the kitchen/nook area. The arrangement of the kitchen and its eating area will create a nostalgic country-kitchen atmosphere. The library can be called upon to serve a multitude of functions. Note powder room and laundry. Upstairs, four big bedrooms and three baths. Also plenty of storage.

Design S 2541

1,985 Sq. Ft.-First Floor/1,659 Sq. Ft.-Second Floor
59,012 Cu. Ft.

Here is English Tudor styling at its stately best. The massive stone work is complemented by stucco and massive beams. The diamond lite windows, the projecting bays, the carriage lamps and the twin chimneys add to the charm of this exterior. The spacious center entrance routes traffic effectively to all areas. Worthy of particular note is the formal living room with its fireplace, the adjacent family room overlooking the terrace, the quiet study with fireplace, two sizeable dining areas, and an excellent master suite.

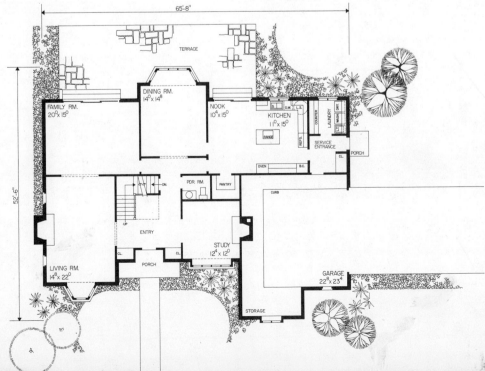

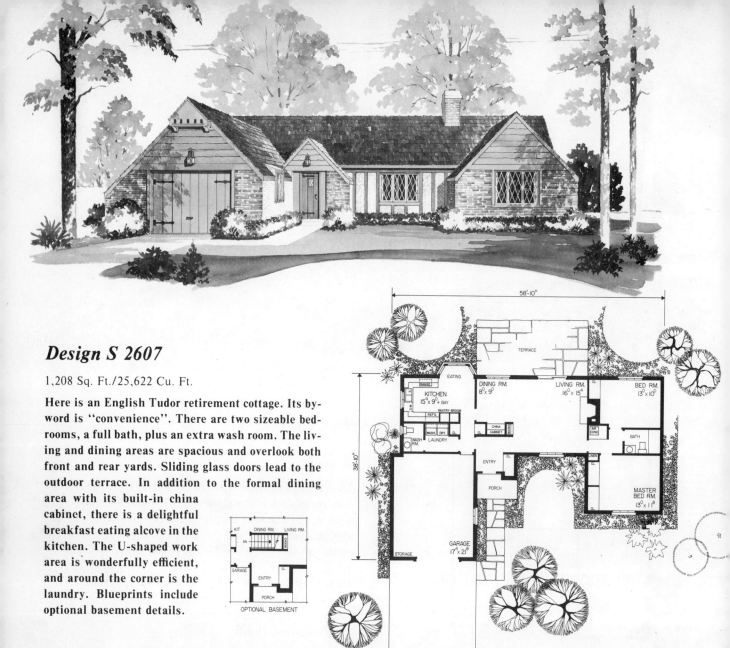

Design S 2607

1,208 Sq. Ft./25,622 Cu. Ft.

Here is an English Tudor retirement cottage. Its by-word is "convenience". There are two sizeable bedrooms, a full bath, plus an extra wash room. The living and dining areas are spacious and overlook both front and rear yards. Sliding glass doors lead to the outdoor terrace. In addition to the formal dining area with its built-in china cabinet, there is a delightful breakfast eating alcove in the kitchen. The U-shaped work area is wonderfully efficient, and around the corner is the laundry. Blueprints include optional basement details.

OPTIONAL BASEMENT

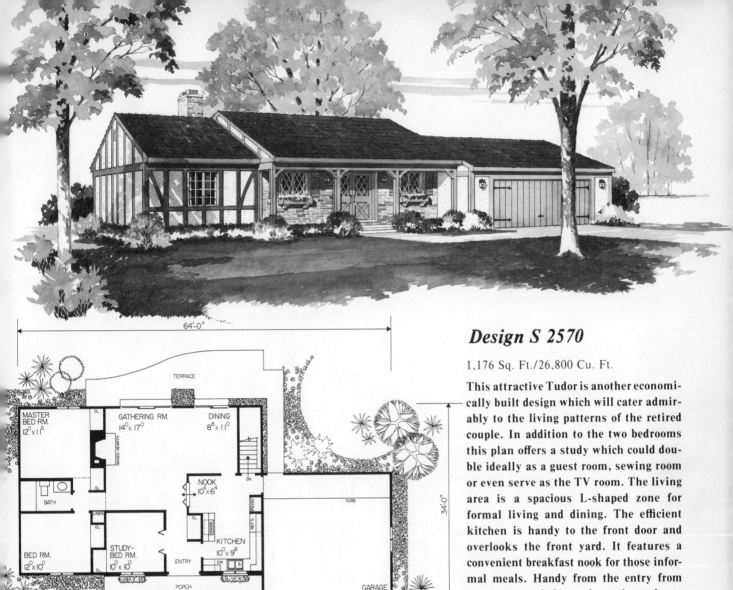

Design S 2570

1,176 Sq. Ft./26,800 Cu. Ft.

This attractive Tudor is another economically built design which will cater admirably to the living patterns of the retired couple. In addition to the two bedrooms this plan offers a study which could double ideally as a guest room, sewing room or even serve as the TV room. The living area is a spacious L-shaped zone for formal living and dining. The efficient kitchen is handy to the front door and overlooks the front yard. It features a convenient breakfast nook for those informal meals. Handy from the entry from the garage and the yard are the stairs to the basement. Don't overlook the attractive front porch.

Design S 2374

1,1919 Sq. Ft./39,542 Cu. Ft.

This English adaptation will never grow old. There is, indeed much here to please the eye. The wavy-edged siding contrasts pleasingly with the diagonal pattern of brick below. The diamond lites of the windows create their own special effect. The projecting brick wall creates a pleasant court outside the covered front porch. The floor plan is well-zoned with the three bedrooms and two baths comprising a distinct sleeping wing. Flanking the entrance hall are the formal living room and the informal, multi-purpose family room. The large dining room is strategically located. The mud room area is adjacent to the extra wash room and the stairs to the basement.

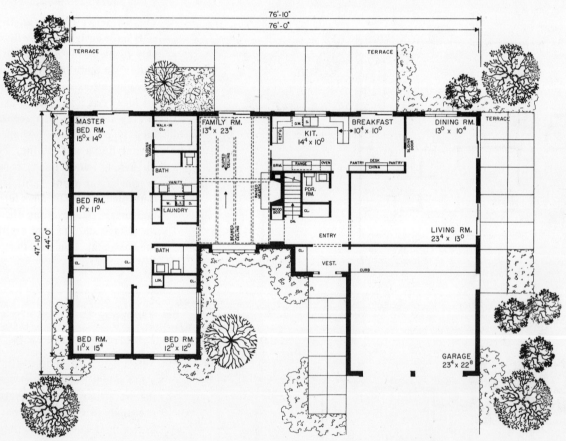

Design S 2142   2,450 Sq. Ft./43,418 Cu. Ft.

Adaptations of Old England have become increasingly popular in to-day's building scene. And little wonder; for many of these homes when well-designed have a very distinctive charm. Here is certainly a home which will be like no other in its neighborhood. Its very shape adds an extra measure of uniqueness. And inside, there is all the livability the exterior seems to foretell. The sleeping wing has four bedrooms, two full baths, and the laundry room—just where the soiled linen originates. The location of the family room is an excellent one. For with children there is usually much traffic between family room and bedrooms. The spacious formal living and dining area will enjoy its privacy and be great fun to furnish.

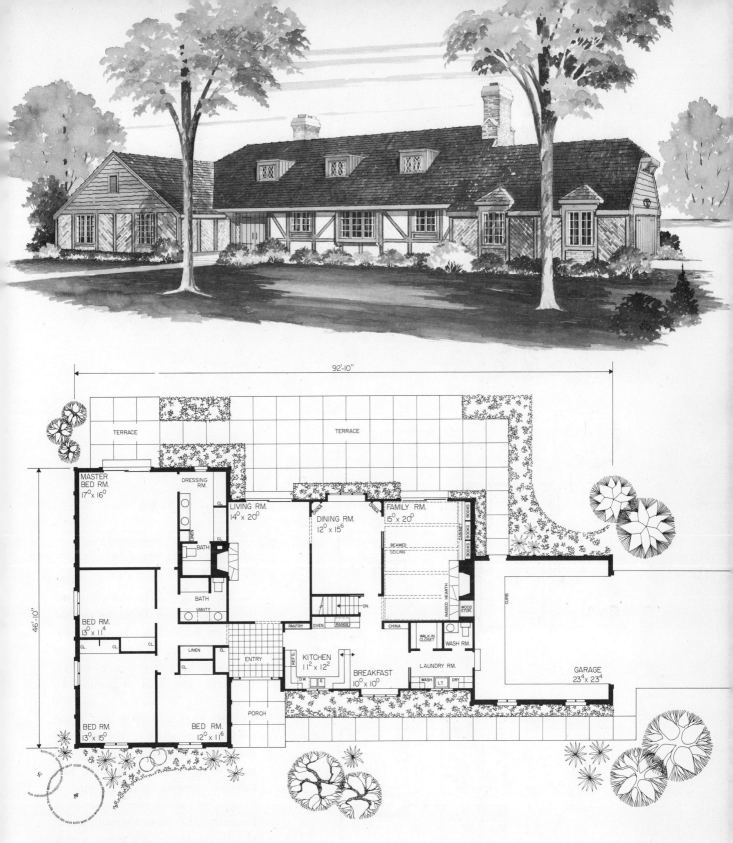

Design S 2378

2,580 Sq. Ft./49,972 Cu. Ft.

If yours is a preference for an exterior that exudes both warmth and formality, the styling of English Tudor may suit your fancy. A host of architectural features blend together to produce this delightfully appealing exterior. Observe the window treatment and the double front doors. Notice the interesting use of contrasting exterior materials. Don't overlook the two stylish chimneys. The manner in which the interior functions to provide the fine living patterns is outstanding. Each of four main rooms-master bedroom, living, dining, and family rooms-look out on the rear terraces. The efficient U-shaped kitchen is strategically located near the front door. There is a complete laundry room with a wash room and a walk-in closet nearby. Folding stairs provide access to the attic.

Design S 2589

1,801 Sq. Ft. — Upper Level
1,061 Sq. Ft. — Lower Level
32,770 Cu. Ft.

An interesting bi-level with a dramatic overhanging upper level. Behind the appealing double front doors is the entry which routes traffic directly to the two levels. Up a short flight of stairs is the main living level. It features the formal living and dining rooms. The efficient kitchen with its fine island work surface opens to the breakfast nook. There are three bedrooms, two baths and good storage facilities. Two balconies provide access to outdoor living. Down another set of stairs from the entry is the lower level with another bedroom (or make it a study), a big family room, a laundry, a full bath and the oversized garage. Don't miss the built-ins, the two fireplaces and the sloped ceiling.

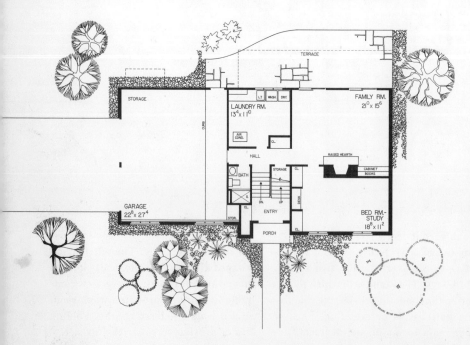

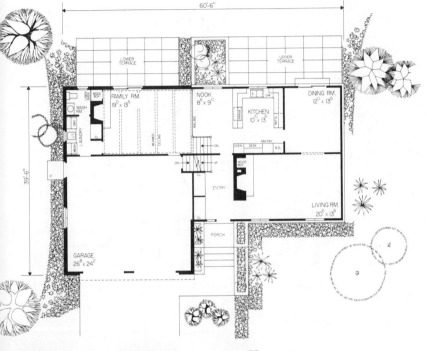

Design S 2624

904 Sq. Ft. — Main Level
404 Sq. Ft. — Lower Level
1,120 Sq. Ft. — Upper Level
39,885 Cu. Ft.

You'll not require a huge piece of land on which to build this impressive tri-level Tudor home. In fact, with the two-car garage conveniently tucked under the upper level you'll be able to get by with a relatively modest building site. The four bedroom level, with its two full baths, good storage and out-door balcony will cater to the needs of the young, growing family. For living activities there is the formal living room and the multi-purpose family room. For dining facilities there is the separate dining room and the pleasant break-fast nook. The efficient, U-shaped kit-chen has good counter and cupboard space. And even a deck, pantry and broom closet. Don't miss the two fire-places and laundry/wash room area. A great house!

47

Design S 2525

919 Sq. Ft. — First Floor
949 Sq. Ft. — Second Floor
29,200 Cu. Ft.

Here is an economically built home that can be constructed with either of the two illustrated exteriors. Which is your favorite? The two study areas provide plenty of multi-purpose, informal living space.

The Pleasing Formality of **French Adaptations**

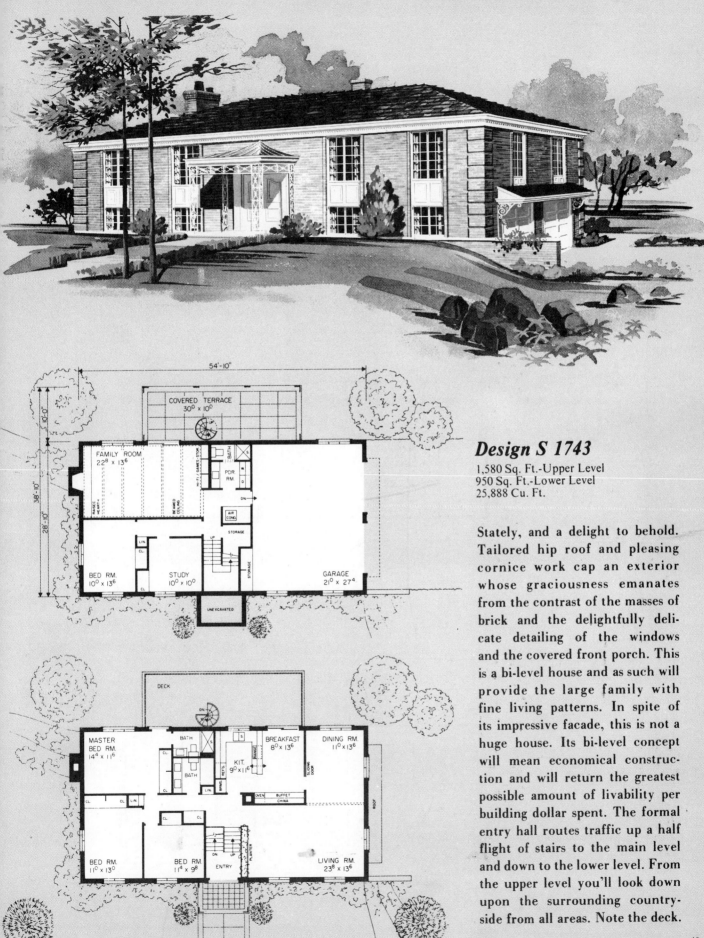

Design S 1743

1,580 Sq. Ft.-Upper Level
950 Sq. Ft.-Lower Level
25,888 Cu. Ft.

Stately, and a delight to behold. Tailored hip roof and pleasing cornice work cap an exterior whose graciousness emanates from the contrast of the masses of brick and the delightfully delicate detailing of the windows and the covered front porch. This is a bi-level house and as such will provide the large family with fine living patterns. In spite of its impressive facade, this is not a huge house. Its bi-level concept will mean economical construction and will return the greatest possible amount of livability per building dollar spent. The formal entry hall routes traffic up a half flight of stairs to the main level and down to the lower level. From the upper level you'll look down upon the surrounding countryside from all areas. Note the deck.

49

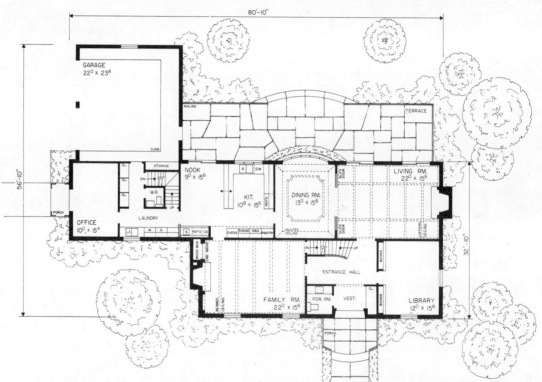

Design S 1839

2,204 Sq. Ft.—First Floor/1,486 Sq. Ft.—Second Floor/330 Sq. Ft.—Maid's Area/55,683 Cu. Ft.

Imagine, five bedrooms, a quiet library, a home office (use it as a first floor hobby room if you perfer), a big family room, a first floor laundry, a maid's suite, and three full baths plus an extra powder room and wash room! Note the large formal living and dining rooms which look out upon the raised terrace.

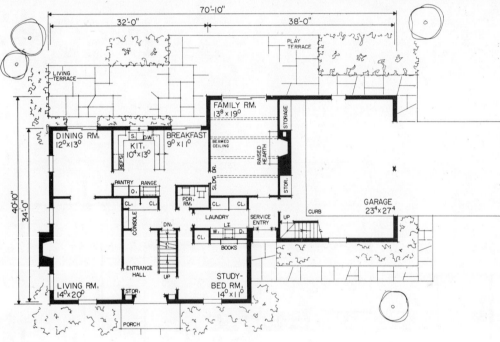

Design S 1934   1,622 Sq. Ft.—First Floor/2,002 Sq. Ft.—Second Floor/51,758 Cu. Ft.

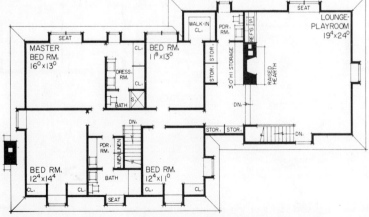

The two-story French Mansard has become a favorite of many during the past few years. Its attractive proportion and pleasing formality have become familiar to most of us. Be sure to observe the fine architectural detailing such as the dentils at the cornice, the brick quoins at the corners, the recessed and paneled front entrance, the carriage lamps, etc. The interior of this home is even more outstanding. Here is a house that could function as a four, five, or even a six bedroom home! And with plenty of space left over for formal and informal living and dining. For efficient housekeeping, there is the U-shaped kitchen and the separate first floor laundry. Observe the central location of powder room. Note hall storage facilities.

Design S 2220   2,646 Sq. Ft./42,578 Cu. Ft.

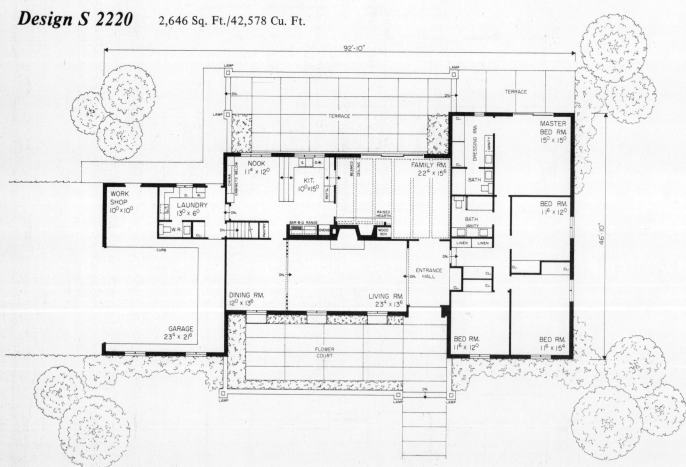

The gracious formality of this home is reminiscent of a popularly accepted French styling. The hip-roof, the brick quoins, the cornice details, the arched window heads, the distinctive shutters, the recessed double front doors, the massive center chimney, and the de-

lightful flower court are all features which set the dramatic appeal of this home. This floor plan is a favorite of many. The four bedroom, two bath sleeping wing is a zone by itself. Further, the formal living and dining rooms are ideally located. For entertaining

they function well together and look out upon the pleasant flower court. Overlooking the raised living terrace at the rear are the family and breakfast rooms and work center. Don't miss the laundry and extra wash room. The big garage and work shop are great.

Design S 2179   2,439 Sq. Ft./33,043 Cu. Ft.

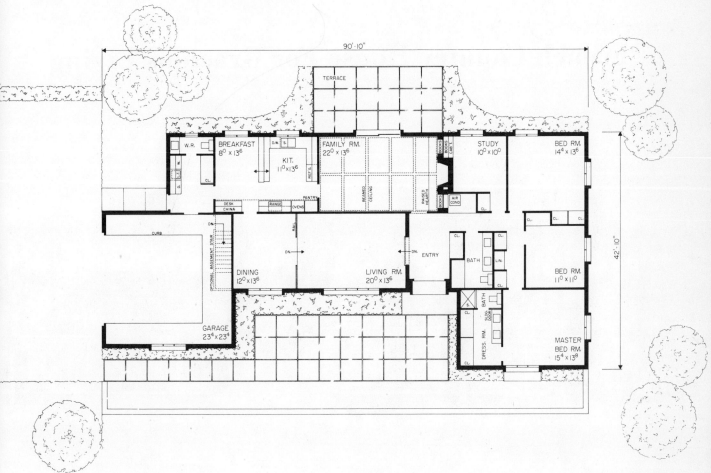

The formality of this French adaptation is a pleasing picture to behold. Wherever you may choose to build it, this one-story will most assuredly receive the accolades of passers-by. It is the outstanding proportion and the fine detail that make this a home of distinction. What's inside is every bit as delightful as what is outside. Your family will enjoy its three sizable bedrooms. The study will be a favorite haven for those who wish a period of peace and quiet. The sunken living room and the informal family room offer two large areas for family living. For eating there are the breakfast and separate dining rooms. Two baths, extra wash room serve family well.

French Country House For Gracious Living

From the graceful, curving drive court to the formal living room, this expansive, hospitable French country house welcomes the visitor. Its stately facade is characterized by the varying roof planes, the brick masses, the quoins, the window treatment, the raised terrace area, and the panelled, recessed front entrance with its double doors. The chimney detail, the cupola, the carriage lamps, and the roof finials add that extra measure of exquisite appeal. The rear elevation with its projecting living room is no less attractive. This will truly be an outstanding home for entertaining. The rooms comprising the living area are large and function well with the formal foyer. Sliding glass doors lead to the rear outdoor terrace development. The formal dining room is well situated.

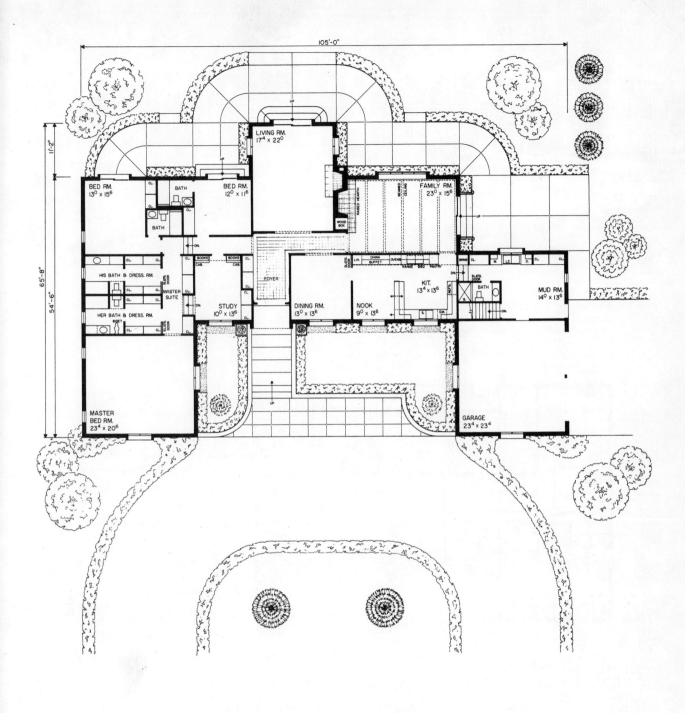

Design S 2212   3,577 Sq. Ft./76,208 Cu. Ft.

The cozy, informal family room highlights a beamed ceiling and a raised hearth fireplace. The U-shaped kitchen with its adjacent breakfast room will be a joy in which to operate. Note the built-in linen closet, the china cupboard, the buffet, the ovens, range and barbecue units, and the pantry. A couple of steps down from the kitchen is the large mud room, a full bath with stall shower, the laundry equipment and excellent storage facilities. From here there is direct access to the big garage. The sleeping wing is also sunken. The master suite highlights separate "his" and "her" baths and dressing rooms, and plenty of wardrobe closets. The study is directly accessible from this fine master suite. Don't miss the other two full baths.

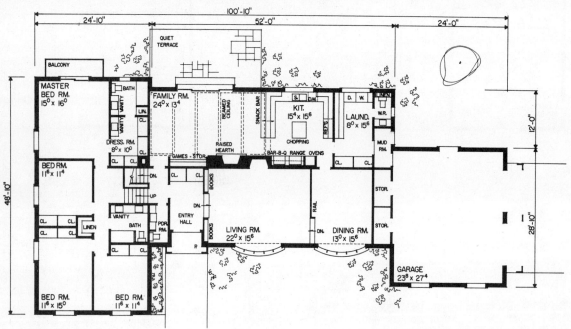

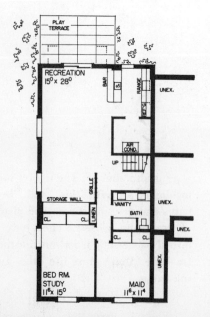

Design S 1270

1,648 Sq. Ft.—Main Level/1,200 Sq. Ft.—Upper Level
1,200 Sq. Ft.—Lower Level/48,856 Cu. Ft.

A French Provincial adaptation with an enormous amount of livability on three levels. Whether called upon to function as a four or six bedroom home, there will be plenty of space in which to move around. Whatever the activities of the family—formal or informal—this floor plan contains the facilities to cater to them. For instance, there is the family room of the main level and the recreation room of the lower level to more than adequately serve informal pursuits. Then there is the sunken living room and the separate dining room for formal entertaining. There are three full baths, a powder room and an extra wash room. The main level laundry will save many steps. There are two fireplaces and exceptional storage facilities. Four bedrooms highlight upper level.

This French adaptation has a finely detailed facade highlighted by such features as brick quoins at the corners, a projected bay window, exquisite double front doors, boxed two-story window frames, small paned windows, and a high-styled chimney. Inside, there are four levels which are sure to make positive contributions to true Convenient Living patterns. The L-shaped living/dining area is a dandy. The kitchen, with its breakfast nook, is spacious. The lower level family room, with its raised hearth fireplace, will be, of course, the most popular spot in the house. Down a few stairs from this level is the basement. Here is all kinds of space for bulk storage and the pursuit of hobbies. Note all those sliding glass doors to terraces and balcony. A canopy shelters garage entrance.

Design S 2291

988 Sq. Ft.-Main Level
1,260 Sq. Ft.-Upper Level
525 Sq. Ft.-Lower Level
35,486 Cu. Ft.

57

Design S 1272

1,690 Sq. Ft./32,588 Cu. Ft.

Designed for the family who want the refinement of French Provincial, but on a small scale. Keynoting its charm are the long shutters, the delightful entrance porch with its wood posts, the interesting angles of the hip roof, and the pair of panneled garage doors. Behind this formal facade is a simple, efficient, up-to-date floor plan. The living patterns for the family occupying this house will be toward the rear where the long living terrace is just a step outside the glass sliding doors of the formal and informal living areas.

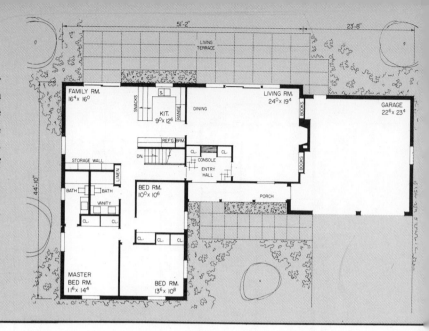

Design S 1797

1,618 Sq. Ft./18,600 Cu. Ft.

A house to be looked at and lived in—that's what this impressively formal French Provincial adaptation represents. The front court, just inside the brick wall with its attractive iron gate, sets the patterns of formality that are so apparent inside. The formal living and dining rooms separate the sleeping area from the kitchen family room area. A pass-thru facilitates serving of informal snacks in family room.

OPTIONAL BASEMENT

Design S 1815

1,592 Sq. Ft./21,365 Cu. Ft.

Delicately arched windows and doors, wrought iron trellis-work, paneled doors, and fine cornice treatment—all mark this house as reminiscent of French Provincial. The covered front porch is another feature not to be overlooked. While the L shape of this house is a distinctive factor in contributing to the exterior design appeal, it is equally important in contributing to outstanding floor planning. Study the zoning. Note how each of the three main areas—formal living and dining, informal kitchen and family, and quiet sleeping—all enjoy their separation from each other.

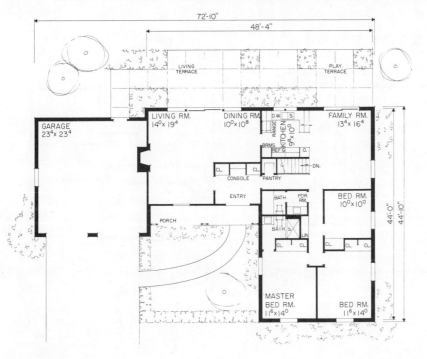

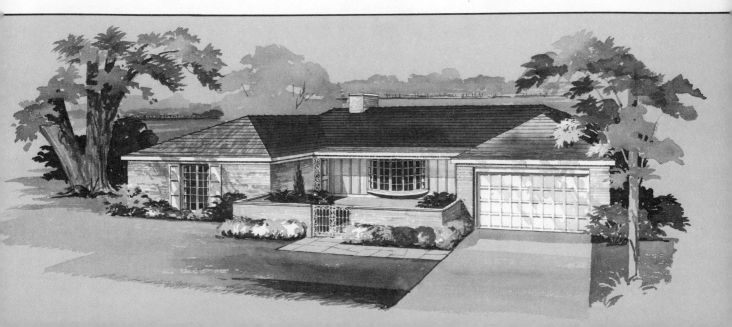

Design S 2543

2,345 Sq. Ft.-First Floor/1,687 Sq. Ft.-Second Floor
76,000 Cu. Ft.

Certainly a dramatic French adaptation highlighted by effective window treatment, delicate cornice detailing, appealing brick quoins, and excellent proportion. Stepping through the double front doors the drama is heightened by the spacious entry hall with its two curving staircases to the second floor. The upper hall is open and looks down to the hall below. There is a study and a big gathering room which looks out on the raised terrace. The work center is outstanding. The garage will accommodate three cars.

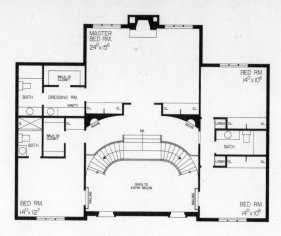

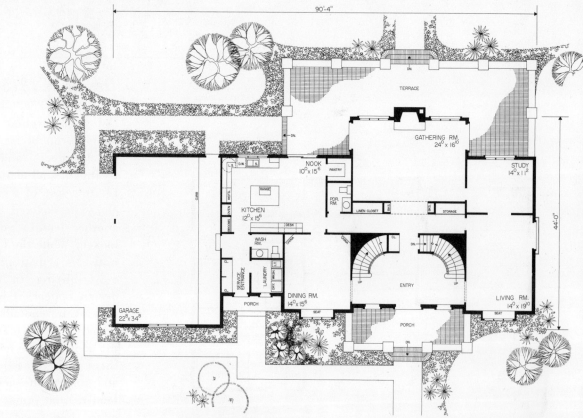

Design S 2376

1,422 Sq. Ft.-First Floor/1,020 Sq. Ft.-Second Floor
38,134 Cu. Ft.

Make your next home one that will be truly distinctive and a reflection of your good taste. This high styled design will surely catch the eye of even the most casual of passers-by. The appealing roof lines, the window treatment, the arched openings and the stucco exterior set the charming character of this two-story. The covered front porch provides sheltered entry to the spacious foyer. From this point traffic patterns flow efficiently to all areas. Notice how the family room/laundry zone is sunken one step. The kitchen is flanked by the two eating areas and they overlook the rear yard. Each of the two large living areas features a fireplace and functions directly through sliding glass door with a covered porch. Upstairs there are four bedrooms, two baths and plenty of closets.

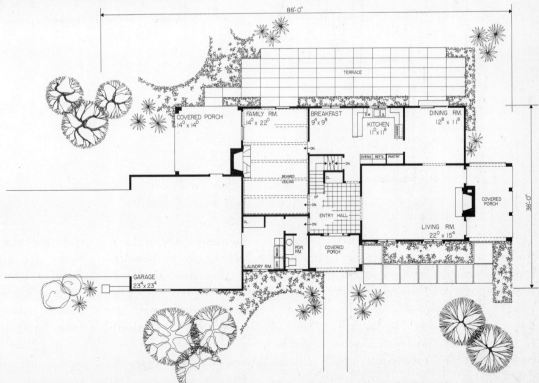

Design S 1874   2,307 Sq. Ft./39,922 Cu. Ft.

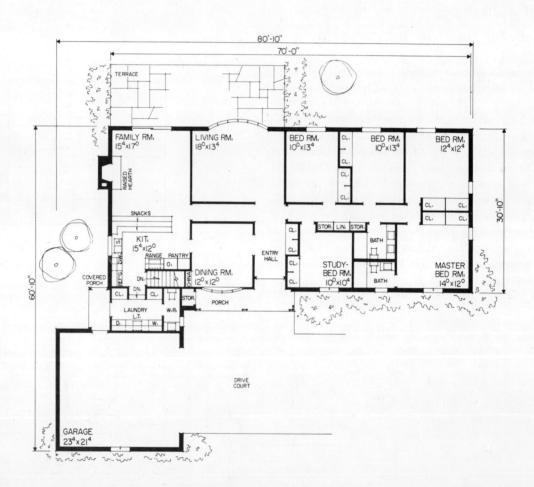

Certainly the exterior of this French adaptation with its hip-roof, its wrought iron, its attractive windows, its brick quoins at the corners, and its cupola, doesn't look familiar. Here is truly good design—in high style. Nor is the interior likely to look very familiar, either. Have you even seen quite the livability this one-story has to offer? There are five bedrooms, 2½ baths, separate dining room, informal family room, efficient kitchen, convenient laundry, and an attached two-car garage. The storage is outstanding. There are plenty of wardrobe closets, linen storage, china cabinet, kitchen cupboards, and laundry cabinets. There is even a storage unit on the covered front porch. The basement offers further storage potential.

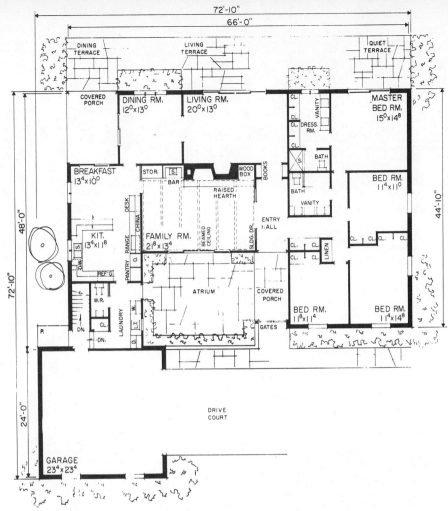

Design S 1881   2,472 Sq. Ft./44,434 Cu. Ft.

Whether you park your car in the garage as the owner of this attractive home, or in the area reserved for guests, you'll be sure to appreciate all that this design has to offer. Its appealing exterior is one which will never grow old. Its practical interior is one which will forever serve the family ideally. When you enter the house from the garage there is a handy closet awaiting your coat. The wash room is nearby. The work center is but a couple of steps beyond with the informal family room just around the corner. On the way to the front door your guests pass the secluded atrium. Once inside they are but a few steps from the family and living rooms. Whether enjoyed to the front or the rear of this home, outdoor living will be gracious, indeed. Note the covered porch and the terraces in the rear. There are three of them!

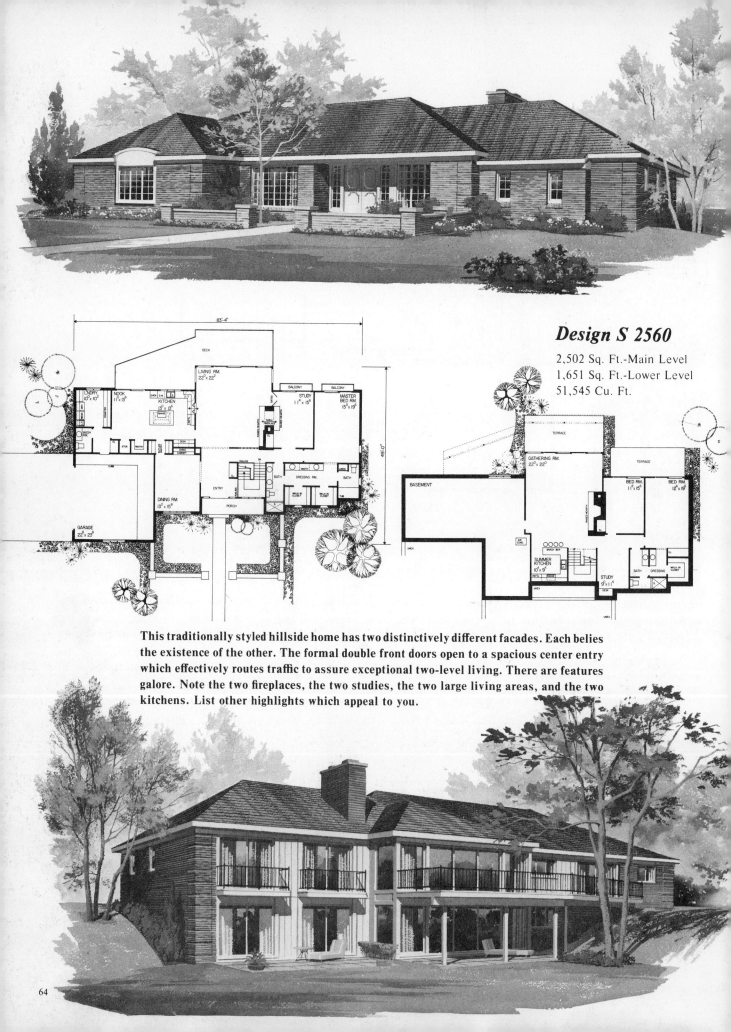

Design S 2560

2,502 Sq. Ft.-Main Level
1,651 Sq. Ft.-Lower Level
51,545 Cu. Ft.

This traditionally styled hillside home has two distinctively different facades. Each belies the existence of the other. The formal double front doors open to a spacious center entry which effectively routes traffic to assure exceptional two-level living. There are features galore. Note the two fireplaces, the two studies, the two large living areas, and the two kitchens. List other highlights which appeal to you.

The Warmth and Charm of Early American Homes

Design S 1987

1,632 Sq. Ft. — First Floor
912 Sq. Ft. — Second Floor
35,712 Cu. Ft.

The comforts of home will be endless when enjoyed in this picturesque Colonial adaptation. And the reasons why are readily apparent. The large family room with its beamed ceiling and raised hearth fireplace functions through sliding glass doors with the big rear terrace. On the other hand, the formal living room is somewhat isolated so as to experience a full measure of privacy. It, also, has a fireplace. The breakfast room and dining room more than adequately service the eating requirements. The extra room — the study — will add mightily to the family's comfort since it can be called upon to serve many functions.

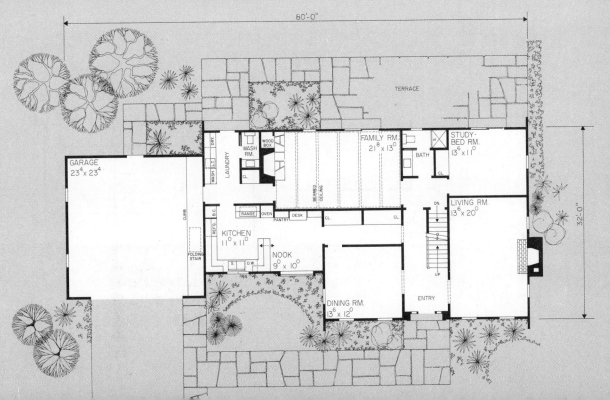

Design S 2539

1,450 Sq. Ft.-First Floor/1,167 Sq. Ft.-Second Floor
46,738 Cu. Ft.

This appealingly proportioned Gambrel exudes an aura of coziness. The beauty of the main part of the house is delightfully symmetrical and is enhanced by the attached garage and laundry room. The center entrance routes traffic directly to all major zones of the house. The efficient kitchen is strategically situated between the formal dining room and the informal breakfast nook with its bay window overlooking the rear yard. The family room is huge and features two sets of sliding glass doors and an attractive raised hearth fireplace. Upstairs, four bedrooms and two full baths.

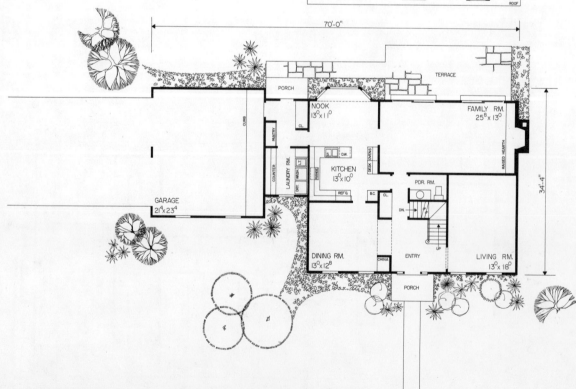

Design S 2538

1,503 Sq. Ft.-First Floor/1,095 Sq. Ft.-Second Floor
44,321 Cu. Ft.

This Salt Box is charming, indeed. The livability it has to offer to the large and growing family is great. The rear dormer of the second floor permits the locations of four bedrooms and two baths. The master suite has a fireplace, dressing area, vanity, and walk-in closet. The entry is spacious and is open to the second floor balcony. For living areas, there is the study in addition to the living and family rooms. The kitchen area, with its island cooking unit and adjacent breakfast nook, will be a favorite gathering spot. Note the laundry room and separate service entrance.

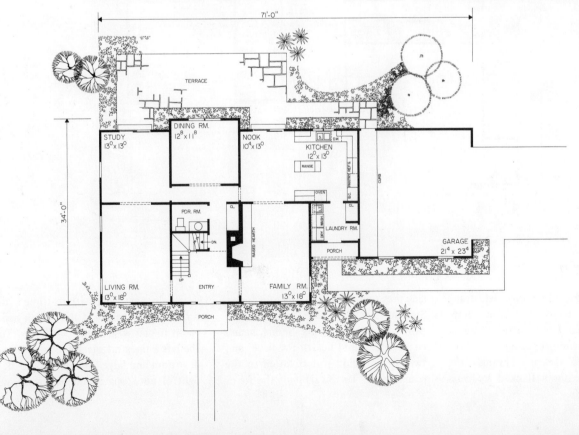

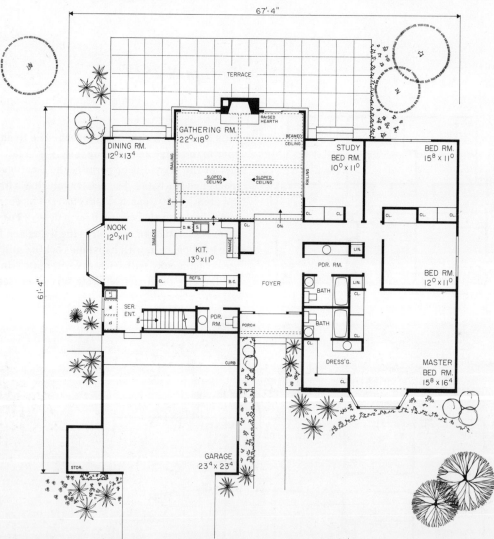

Design S 2527 2,392 Sq. Ft. / 42,579 Cu. Ft.

Vertical boards and battens, fieldstone, bay window, a dovecote, a gas lamp, and a recessed front entrance are among the appealing exterior features of this U-shaped design. Through the double front doors flanked by glass side lites one enters the spacious foyer. Straight ahead is the cozy sunken gathering room with its sloping, beamed ceiling, raised hearth fireplace, and two sets of sliding glass doors to the rear terrace. To the right of the foyer is the sleeping wing with its three bedrooms, study (make it the fourth bedroom if you wish), and two baths. To the left is the strategically located powder room and large kitchen with its delightful nook space and bay window.

What a pleasing, traditional exterior. And what a fine, Convenient Living interior! The configuration of this home leads to interesting roof planes and even functional outdoor terrace areas. The front court and the covered porch with its stolid pillars strike an enchanting note. The gathering room will be just that. It will be the family's multi-purpose living area. Sunken to a level of two steps its already spacious feeling is enhanced by its open planning with the dining room and study. This latter room may be closed off for more privacy if desired. Just adjacent to the foyer is the open stairwell to the basement level. Here will be the possibility of developing recreation space.

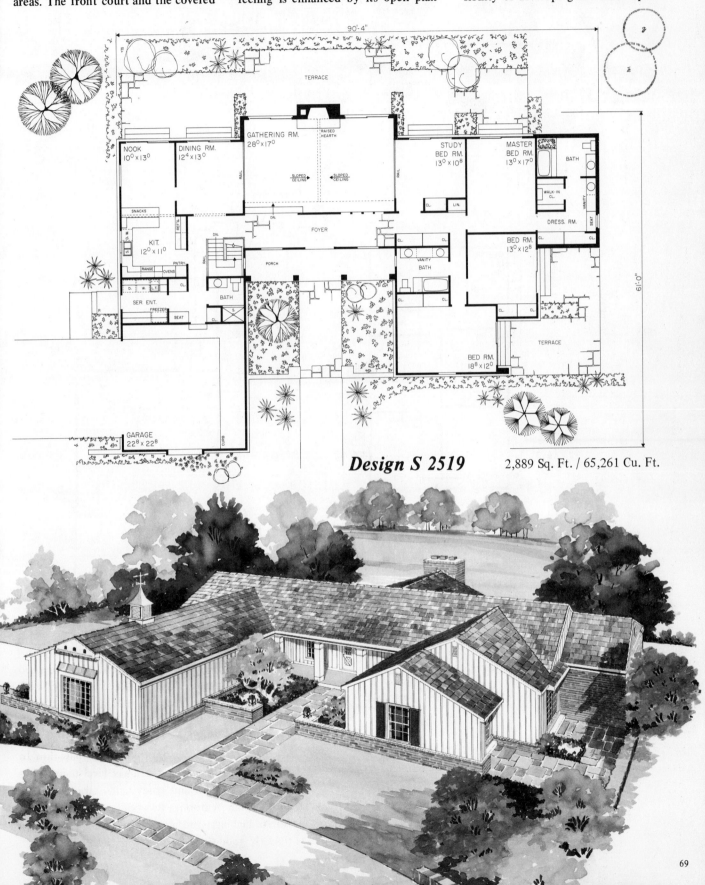

Design S 2519   2,889 Sq. Ft. / 65,261 Cu. Ft.

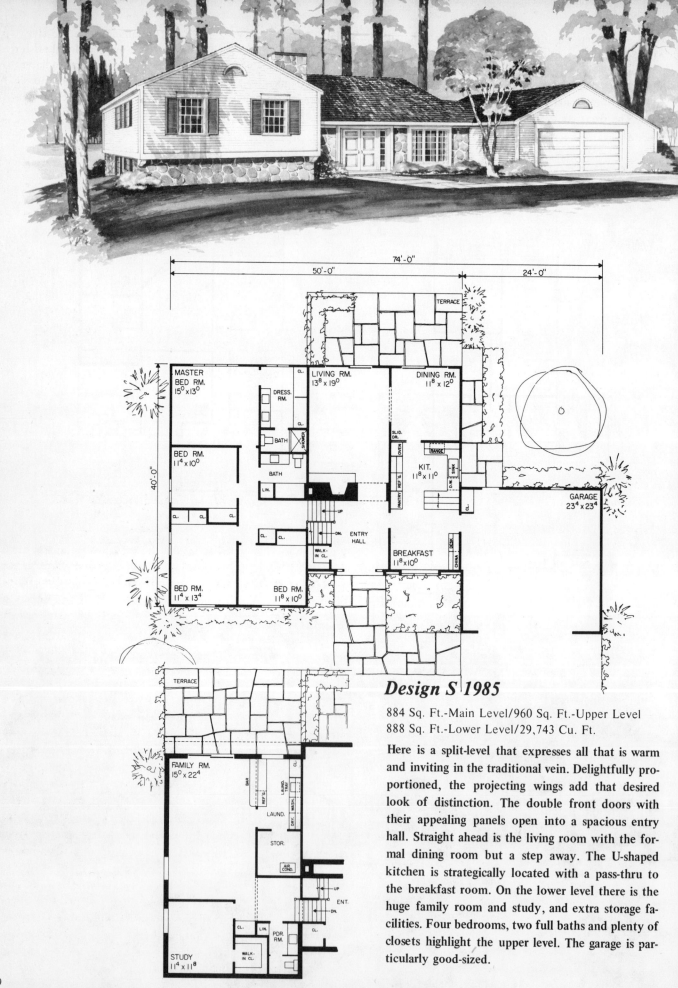

74'-0"
50'-0" **24'-0"**

TERRACE

MASTER BED RM. 15⁰ x 13⁰

DRESS. RM.

LIVING RM. 13⁸ x 19⁰

DINING RM. 11⁸ x 12⁰

BATH

BED RM. 11⁴ x 10⁰

SHOWER

BATH

40'-0"

LIN.

SLID. DR.

OVEN

RANGE

PANTRY

REF'G.

KIT. 11⁸ x 11⁰

SINK

D.W.

cl.

GARAGE 23⁴ x 23⁴

CL. CL. CL.

UP

CL. CL.

DN.

ENTRY HALL

WALK-IN CL.

BED RM. 11⁴ x 13⁴

BED RM. 11⁸ x 10⁰

BREAKFAST 11⁸ x 10⁰

DESK

CHINA

TERRACE

FAMILY RM. 15⁰ x 22⁴

BAR

REF'G.

LAUND. TRAY

WASH.

DRY.

CL.

LAUND.

STOR.

AIR COND.

UP

ENT.

DN.

CL. LIN. PDR. RM.

STUDY 11⁴ x 11⁸

WALK-IN CL.

CL.

Design S 1985

884 Sq. Ft.-Main Level/960 Sq. Ft.-Upper Level
888 Sq. Ft.-Lower Level/29,743 Cu. Ft.

Here is a split-level that expresses all that is warm
and inviting in the traditional vein. Delightfully proportioned, the projecting wings add that desired
look of distinction. The double front doors with
their appealing panels open into a spacious entry
hall. Straight ahead is the living room with the formal dining room but a step away. The U-shaped
kitchen is strategically located with a pass-thru to
the breakfast room. On the lower level there is the
huge family room and study, and extra storage facilities. Four bedrooms, two full baths and plenty of
closets highlight the upper level. The garage is particularly good-sized.

Design S 2216

1,183 Sq. Ft. — Main Level
1,344 Sq. Ft. — Upper Level
659 Sq. Ft. — Lower Level
51,856 Cu. Ft.

What a delightful Colonial adaptation!
Its pleasing proportions and effective use
of horizontal siding and stone contribute
to the appeal. The interesting facade is
enhanced by the projecting wing which
comprises the lower and upper levels. The
covered screen porch is also a handsome
design feature. Properly oriented and enclosed this would be an ideal sun porch
during the cooler months of the year. The
living and dining rooms of the main level
are spacious and feature a bowed bay
window. The kitchen features an island
work center and opens to the informal
breakfast nook. Upstairs there are three
bedroom plus a lounge or study. There
are two full baths on this level along with
the powder room just a few steps from
the main level entrance hall. The master
bedroom has plenty of wardrobe facilities, a dressing room, private bath, and
even a balcony. Then, there is the lower
level family room, a separate laundry area
and another bath. A fourth level is devot-
ed to the basement. It is accessible from
the large two-car garage.

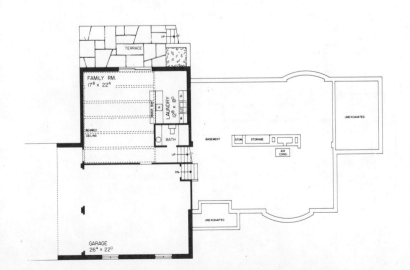

Design S 2610   1,505 Sq. Ft.-First Floor/1,344 Sq. Ft.-Second Floor/45,028 Cu. Ft.

This full two-story traditional will be worthy of note wherever built. It strongly recalls images of a New England of yesteryear. And well it might; for the window treatment is delightful. The front entrance detail is inviting. The narrow horizontal siding and the corner boards are appealing as are the two massive chimneys. The center entrance hall is large with a handy powder room nearby. The study has built-in bookshelves and offers a full measure of privacy. The interior kitchen has a pass-thru to the family room and enjoys all that natural light from the bay window of the nook. A beamed ceiling, fireplace, and sliding glass doors are features of the family room. The mud room highlights a closet, laundry equipment, and an extra wash room. Study the upstairs with those four bedrooms, two baths and plenty of closets.

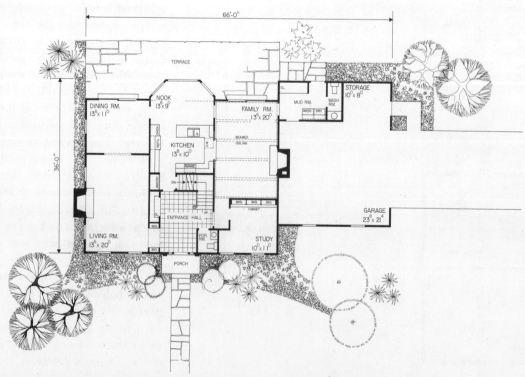

Design S 2368   1,592 Sq. Ft.-First Floor/1,255 Sq. Ft.-Second Floor/54,516 Cu. Ft.

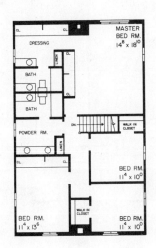

Reminiscent of the old Georgian farmhouses of Colonial America, this home projects an aura of both stateliness and warmth. The main living areas comprise essentially a two-story rectangle. The connecting link to the garage is the spacious family room. Notice that this room with its beamed ceiling and raised hearth fireplace, enjoys a view of both front and rear yards. The 27 foot living room will be a positive delight to furnish. The kitchen will be just great in which to work. With its adjacent breakfast area it, too, will be spacious. Upstairs, there are fine sleeping and bath facilities. Particularly noteworthy, is the extra powder room. For the development of additional livability and storage facilities there is the basement. Don't miss the laundry. This convenient little room will chase wash day blues.

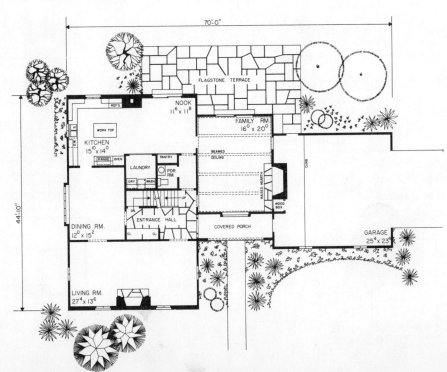

Design S 2569

1,102 Sq. Ft.-First Floor/764 Sq. Ft.-Second Floor
29,600 Cu. Ft.

What an enchanting updated version of the popular Cape Cod cottage. There are facilities for both formal and informal living pursuits. Note first floor laundry.

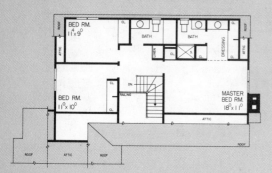

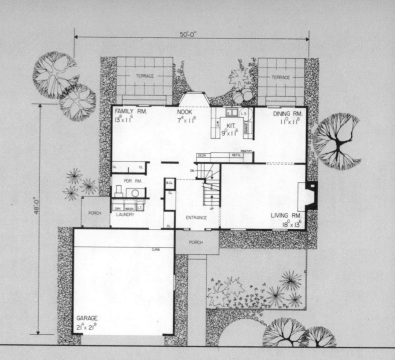

Design S 2559

1,388 Sq. Ft.-First Floor/809 Sq. Ft.-Second Floor
36,400 Cu. Ft.

Imagine, a 26 foot living room with fireplace, a quiet study with built-in bookshelves, and excellent dining facilities. Within such an appealing exterior, too.

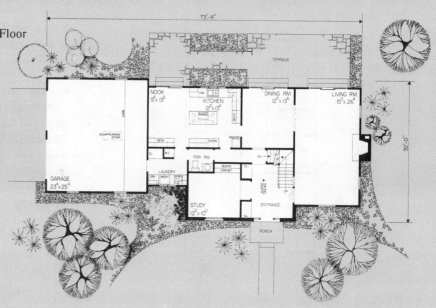

Design S 2563

1,500 Sq. Ft.-First Floor/690 Sq. Ft.-Second Floor
38,243 Cu. Ft.

You'll have all kinds of fun deciding just how your family will function in this dramatically expanded half-house. There is lots of attic storage, too. Observe three-car garage.

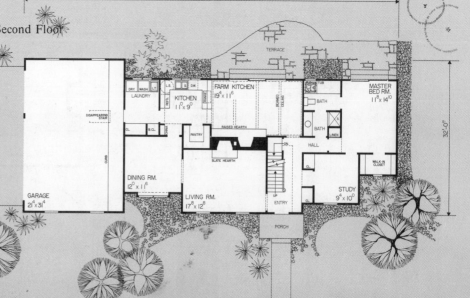

Design S 2181

2,612 Sq. Ft. / 45,230 Cu. Ft.

Here is a rambling traditionally styled ranch home that differs only slightly from its counterpart on the opposing page. It is slightly larger in size and, of course, has its floor plan reversed from left to right. It is hard to imagine a home with any more eye-appeal than this one. It is the complete picture of charm. The interior is no less outstanding. Sliding glass doors permit the large master bedroom, the quiet living room, and the all-purpose family room to function directly with the outdoors.

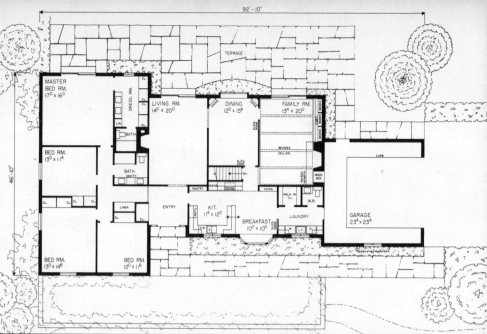

Design S 2316

2,000 Sq. Ft. / 25,242 Cu. Ft.

Here is a basic floor plan which is the favorite of many. It provides for the location, to the front of the plan, of the more formal areas (living and dining rooms); while the informal areas (family room and kitchen) are situated to the rear of the plan and function with the terrace. To the left of the center entrance is the four bedroom, two bath sleeping zone. Adjacent to the kitchen is the utility room with a wash room nearby. The garage features a storage room and work shop.

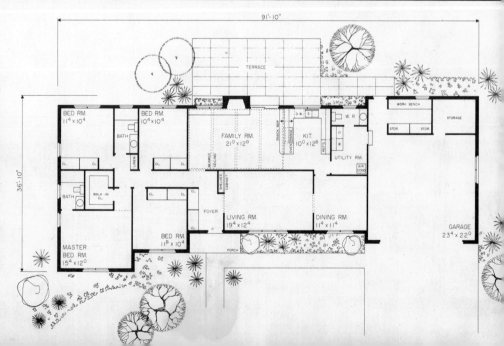

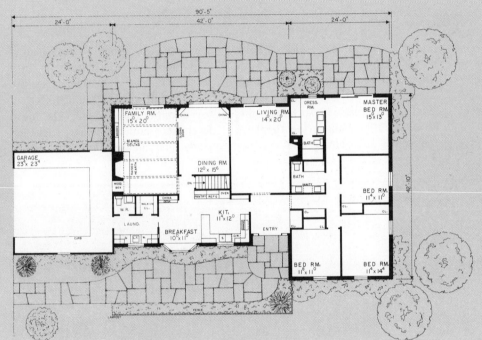

Design S 2144

2,432 Sq. Ft. / 42,519 Cu. Ft.

Have you ever wished you lived in a house in which the living, dining, and family rooms all looked out upon the rear terrace? Further, have you ever wished your home had its kitchen located to the front so that you could see approaching callers? Or, have you ever wished for a house where traffic in from the garage was stopped right in the laundry so that wet, snowy, dirty, and muddy apparel could be shed immediately? If these have been your wishes, this plan may be just for you.

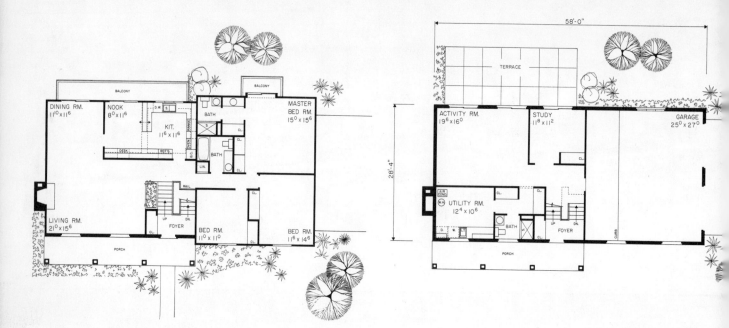

This appealing Colonial adaptation will return to its occupants the utmost in pride of ownership and total livability for the investment dollar. The foundation of this bi-level home is a perfect rectangle and that means economical construction. The sleeping area projects over the garage to pick-up extra livable square footage. The balcony of the master bedroom is a fine feature. The L-shaped living-dining area is spacious and pleasing with such highlights as the built-in planter, the fireplace, the pair of double-hung windows, and the sliding glass doors to the balcony. With nook and the balcony in such proximity, and the kitchen nearby, there will be many a cup of coffee enjoyed out-of-doors. Study the lower level. Here, both the activity room and study function with outdoor terrace.

Impressive? Indeed it is, and with good reason. This finely proportioned exterior is a good example of traditional detailing. The effective window treatment, the front entrance, the overhanging roof supported by the graceful columns, and the horizontal lines of the wood siding all go into making this a most picturesque home. Like most bi-levels it will be economical to build. Particularly noteworthy are such features as the master bedroom with its private bath, the kitchen eating space, the large formal dining area, the upper outdoor deck, the separate laundry room, the fourth bedroom, and the family room. Blueprints for this design include details for building an alternate elevation with a front opening garage and an optional fireplace in the living room, as well as the lower level family room.

Design S 2514   1,713 Sq. Ft. — Upper Level / 916 Sq. Ft. — Lower Level / 32,000 Cu. Ft.

Design S 1341   1,248 Sq. Ft. — Upper Level/676 Sq. Ft. — Lower Level/19, 812 Cu. Ft.

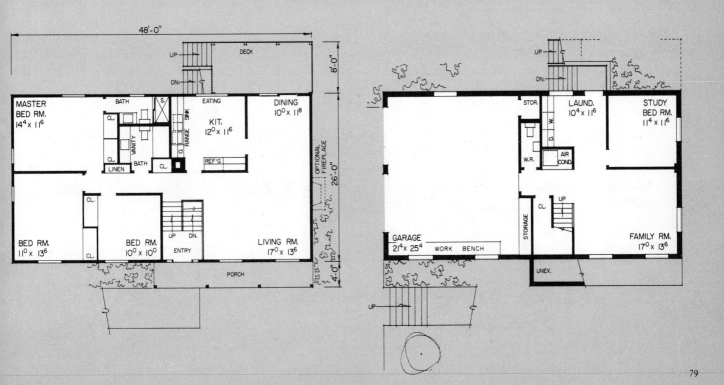

48'-0"

UP
DECK
DN

8'-0"

MASTER BED RM. 14⁴ x 11⁶
BATH
CL.
VANITY
S.
EATING
RANGE
SINK
KIT. 12⁰ x 11⁶
DINING 10⁰ x 11⁸

26'-0"

OPTIONAL FIREPLACE

CL.
CL.
LINEN
BATH
CL.
REF'G

BED RM. 11⁰ x 13⁶
CL.
CL.
BED RM. 10⁰ x 10⁰
UP DN.
ENTRY
LIVING RM. 17⁰ x 13⁶

4'-0"

PORCH

UP
DN.

STOR.
LAUND. 10⁴ x 11⁶
STUDY BED RM. 11⁴ x 11⁶

W.R.
AIR COND.
D. W.

GARAGE 21⁴ x 25⁴   WORK BENCH
STORAGE
CL.
UP
FAMILY RM. 17⁰ x 13⁶

UNEX.

UP

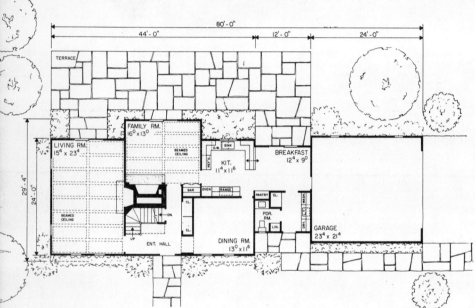

Design S 2101

1,338 Sq. Ft. — First Floor
1,114 Sq. Ft. — Second Floor
39,617 Cu. Ft.

Design S 2191

1,553 Sq. Ft. — First Floor
1,197 Sq. Ft. — Second Floor
47,906 Cu. Ft.

First Floor:

PORCH

FAMILY RM. 16⁰ x 17⁰

KITCHEN 11⁴ x 15⁶

NOOK 12⁰ x 9⁸

BEAMED CEILING

BAR

OVENS   RANGE

PANTRY

DINING 15⁴ x 11⁶

PDR. RM.

LAUNDRY

GARAGE 23⁴ x 23⁴

LIVING RM. 15⁴ x 23⁴

UP   ENTRANCE HALL

FOYER

80'-0"

36'-0"

Second Floor:

WALK-IN CL.

BATH

BATH

STOR.

BED RM. 13⁰ x 11⁶

SEAT   LINEN

MASTER BED RM. 15⁴ x 16⁴

OPEN STAIRWELL

DN.

BED RM. 13⁰ x 13⁰

LOUNGE

SEAT

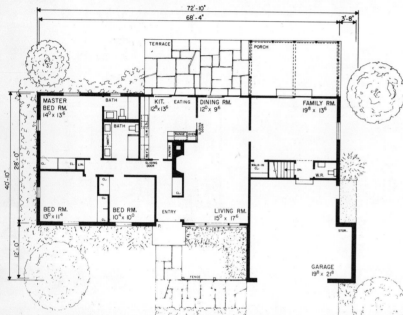

Design S 1100

1,752 Sq. Ft./34,304 Cu. Ft.

This modest sized, brick veneer home has a long list of things in its favor—from its appealing exterior to its feature-packed interior. All of the elements of its exterior complement each other to result in a symphony of attractive design. The floor plan features three bedrooms, two full baths, and extra wash room, a family room, kitchen eating space, a formal dining area, two sets of sliding glass doors to the terrace and one set to the covered porch, built-in cooking equipment, a pantry, and a vanity with twin lavatories. Further, there is the living room fireplace, and attached two-car garage with a bulk storage unit, and a basement for extra storage and miscellaneous recreational activities. A fine investment.

This is truly a prize-winner! The traditional, L-shaped exterior with its flower court and covered front porch is picturesque, indeed. The formal front entry routes traffic directly to the three distinctly zoned areas—the quiet sleeping area; the spacious, formal living and dining area; the efficient, informal family-kitchen. A closer look at the floor plan reveals four bedrooms, two full baths, good storage facilities, a fine snack bar, and sliding glass doors to the rear terrace.

The family-kitchen is ideally located. In addition to being but a few steps from both front and rear entrances, it also affords the housewife a view of both yards. Blueprints include basement and non-basement details.

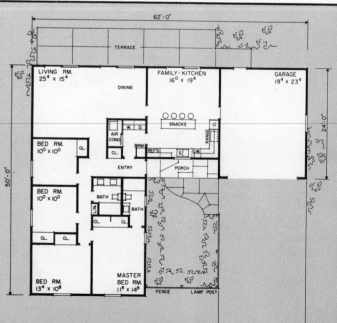

Design S 1343

1,620 Sq. Ft./18,308 Cu. Ft.

Design S 1896

1,690 Sq. Ft./19,435 Cu. Ft.

Complete family livability is provided by this exceptional floor plan. Further, this design has a truly delightful traditional exterior. The fine layout features a center entrance hall with storage closet in addition to the wardrobe closet. Then, there is the formal, front living room and the adjacent, separate dining room. The U-shaped kitchen has plenty of counter and cupboard space. There is even a pantry. The family room functions with the kitchen and is but a step from the outdoor terrace. The mud room has space for storage and laundry equipment. The extra wash room is nearby. The large family will find those four bedrooms and two full baths just the answer to sleeping and bath accommodations. Note optional basement.

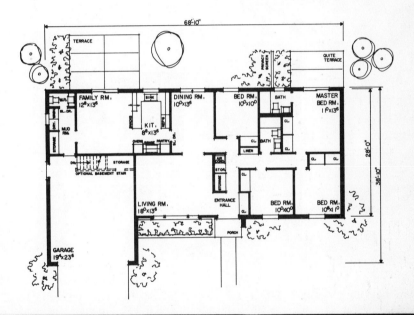

Design S 1355 864 Sq. Ft.–Upper Level/864 Sq. Ft.–Lower Level/16,920 Cu. Ft.

Design S 1822 1,952 Sq. Ft.–Upper Level/1,150 Sq. Ft.–Lower Level/33,280 Cu. Ft.

Design S 1349 1,092 Sq. Ft.–Upper Level/1,092 Sq. Ft.–Lower Level/21,573 Cu. Ft.

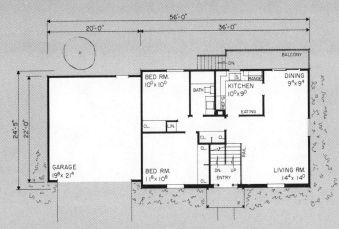
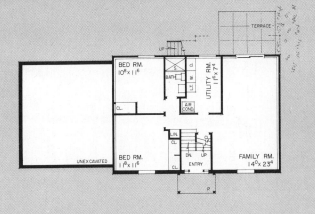

An economically built Colonial bi-level with an exceptional amount of living space. Here is your best possible return on your construction dollar. Under a relatively small roof and on a similar foundation there's over 1,700 square feet. It is used to provide four bedrooms, two baths, a 23 foot family room, a spacious living and dining area, an L-shaped kitchen with eating space, good closet facilities, and a utility room. Everyone will enjoy the balcony off the dining room. There is a terrace off the family room. Sliding glass doors provide the access.

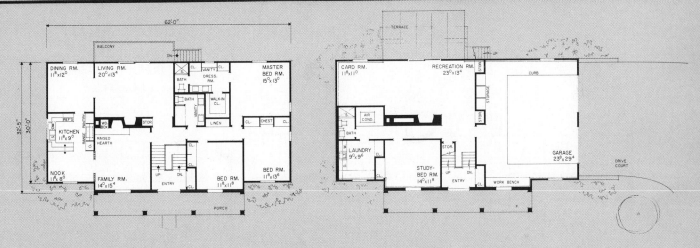

Here is an unique bi-level. Not only in its delightful exterior appeal, but in its practical planning. The covered porch with its impressive columns, the contrasting use of materials, the traditional window and door detailing, are all features which will surely provoke comment from passers-by. The upper level is a complete living unit of three bedrooms, two baths, separate living, dining, and family rooms, a kitchen with eating area, two fireplaces, and an outdoor balcony. The lower level represents bright and cheerful extra living space.

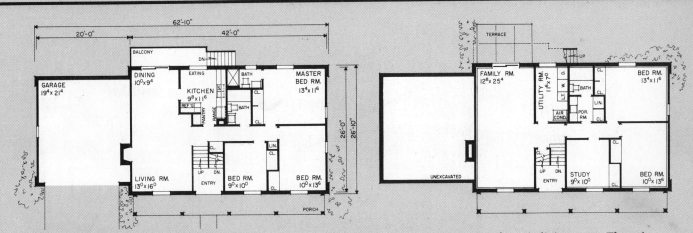

Just think, six bedrooms! Or five bedrooms and a study, or any other kind of combination you might want. If you wanted to enlarge the master bedroom into a suite of rooms this would be entirely possible. And not a bad idea either. However, if you have a lot of children and want plenty of low-cost space this bi-level should fill the bill. There is kitchen eating space and a formal dining area. There is a 25 foot family room, a utility room, and there are three full baths. The upper level balcony will be a lot of fun.

Design S 2157

1,720 Sq. Ft.-First Floor
1,205 Sq. Ft.-Second Floor
40,963 Cu. Ft.

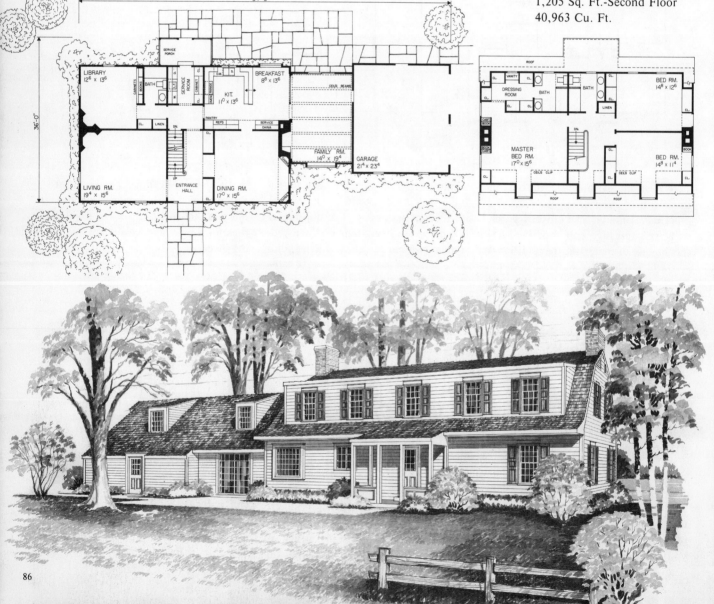

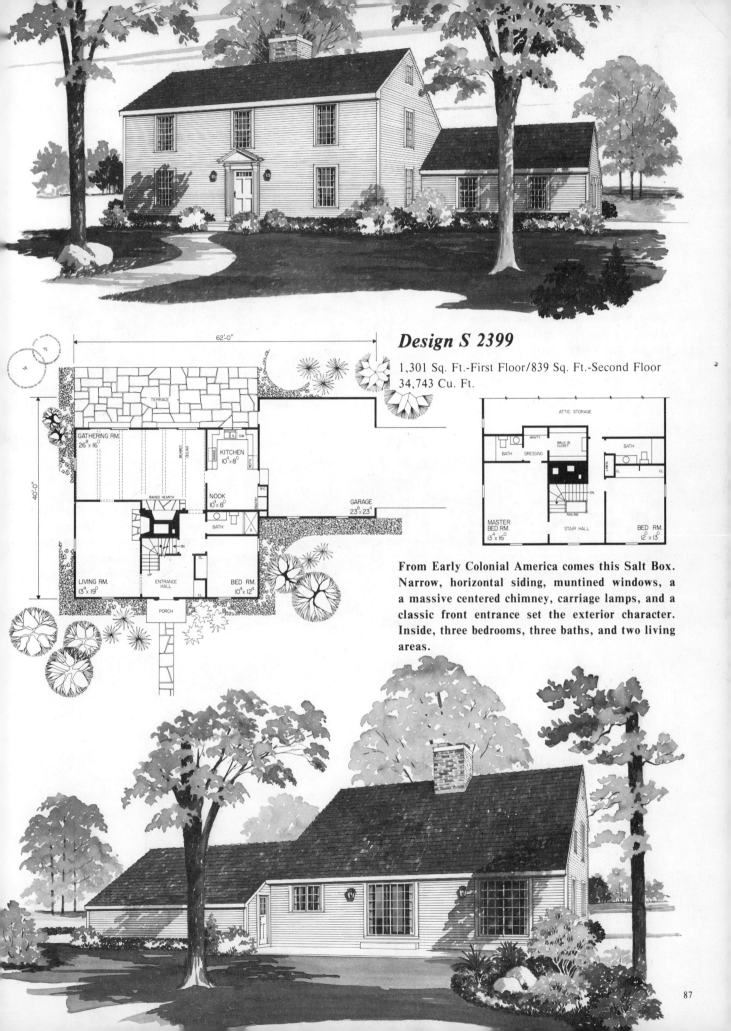

Design S 2399

1,301 Sq. Ft.-First Floor/839 Sq. Ft.-Second Floor
34,743 Cu. Ft.

From Early Colonial America comes this Salt Box. Narrow, horizontal siding, muntined windows, a a massive centered chimney, carriage lamps, and a classic front entrance set the exterior character. Inside, three bedrooms, three baths, and two living areas.

62'-0"

40'-0"

TERRACE

GATHERING RM.
26⁸ x 16⁰

KITCHEN
10⁴ x 8⁰

NOOK
10⁴ x 8⁰

BATH

RAISED HEARTH

GARAGE
23⁴ x 23⁴

LIVING RM.
13⁴ x 19⁰

ENTRANCE HALL

BED RM.
10⁴ x 12⁴

PORCH

UP

DN

CL

CL

ATTIC STORAGE

BATH

VANITY

DRESSING

WALK IN CLOSET

BATH

LINEN

CL

CL

MASTER BED RM.
13⁴ x 16⁰

STAIR HALL

RAILING

DN

BED RM.
12⁰ x 13⁰

Design S 2505

1,366 Sq. Ft. / 29,329 Cu. Ft.

This design offers you a choice of three distinctively different exteriors. Which is your favorite? Blueprints show details for all three optional elevations.

A study of the floor plan reveals a fine measure of livability. In less than 1,400 square feet there are features galore. An excellent return on your construction dollar.

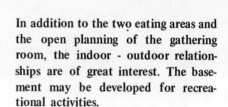

In addition to the two eating areas and the open planning of the gathering room, the indoor - outdoor relationships are of great interest. The basement may be developed for recreational activities.

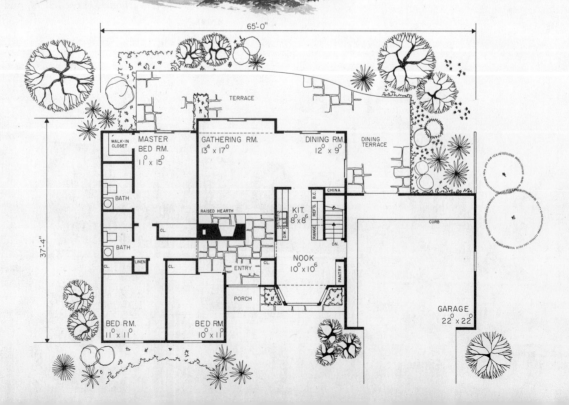

The Rugged Appeal of Spanish & Western Designs

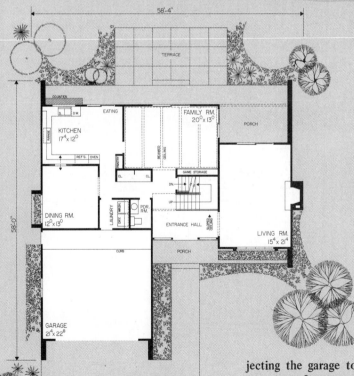

Design S 2390
1,368 Sq. Ft. — First Floor
1,428 Sq. Ft. — Second Floor
37,734 Cu. Ft.

If yours is a large family and you like the architecture of the Far West don't look further. Particularly if you envision building on a modest sized lot. Projecting the garage to the front contributes to the drama of this contemporary two-story. Its stucco exterior is beautifully enhanced by the clay tiles of the varying roof surfaces. Inside the double front doors is just about everything a large, active family would require for pleasurable, convenient living. The focal point, of course, is the five bedroom (count 'em), three bath second floor. Four bedrooms have access to the outdoor balcony. The first floor offers two large living areas — the formal living and informal family living rooms — plus, two eating areas. Although there is the basement, the laundry is on the first floor.

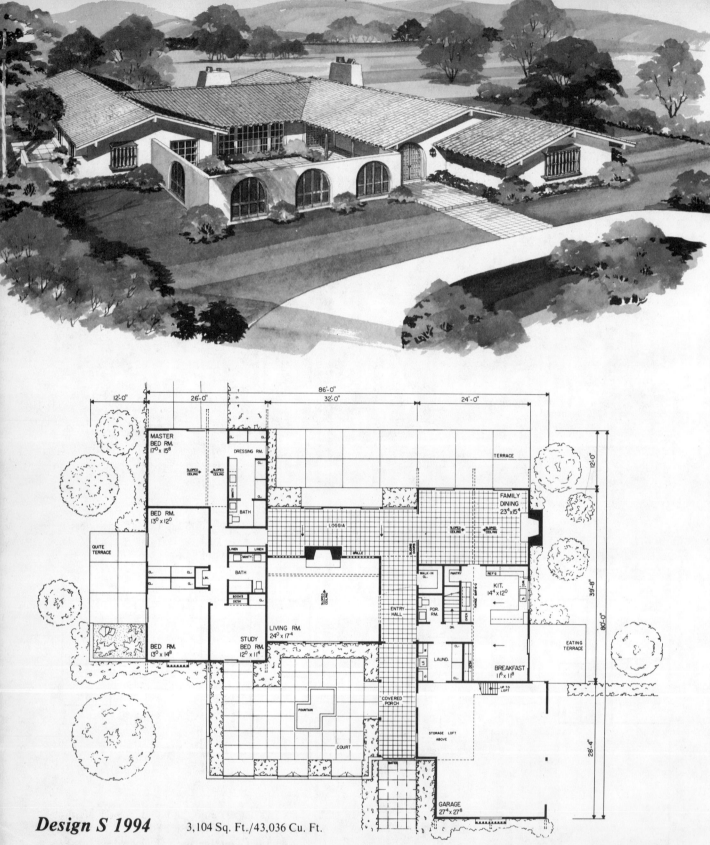

Design S 1994

3,104 Sq. Ft./43,036 Cu. Ft.

The Spanish flavor of the old Southwest is delightfully captured by this sprawling ranch house. Its L-shape and high privacy wall go together to form a wide open interior court. This will be a great place to hold those formal and/or informal garden parties. The plan itself is wonderfully zoned. The center portion of the house is comprised of the big, private living room with sloped ceiling. Traffic patterns will noiselessly skirt this formal living area. The two wings—the sleeping and informal living—are connected by the well-lighted and spacious loggia. In the sleeping wing, observe the size of the various rooms and the fine storage. In the informal living wing, note the big family room and breakfast room.

Design S 2335 2,641 Sq. Ft. / 41,549 Cu. Ft.

Surely a winner for those who have a liking for the architecture of the Far West. With or without the enclosure of the front court, this home with its stucco exterior, brightly colored roof tiles, and exposed rafter tails will be impressive, indeed. The floor plan re-flects a wonderfully zoned interior. This results in a fine separation of func-tions which helps assure Convenient Living. The traffic patterns which flow from the spacious foyer are most ef-ficient. Study them. While the sleeping wing is angled to the front line of the house, the sunken living room pro-jects, at an angle, from the rear. Worthy of particular notice are such highlights as the two covered porches, the raised hearth fireplaces, the first floor laun-dry, the partial basement, and the over-sized garage with storage space.

Design S 2518

1,630 Sq. Ft. — First Floor
1,260 Sq. Ft. — Second Floor
43,968 Cu. Ft.

For those who have a predilection for the Spanish influence in their architecture. Outdoor oriented, each of the major living areas on the first floor have direct access to the terraces. Traffic patterns are excellent.

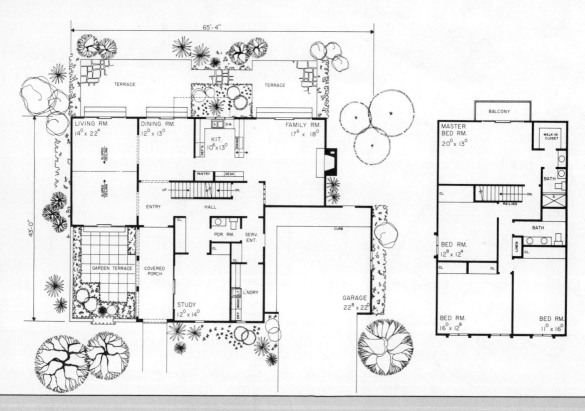

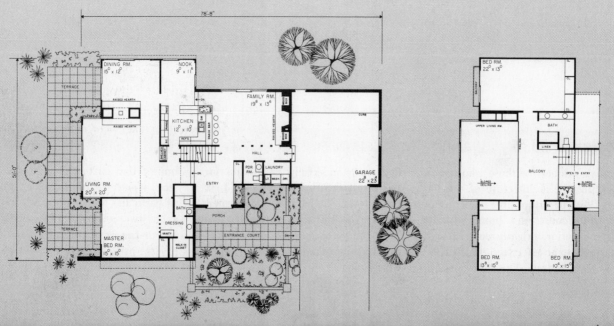

Design S 2517

1,767 Sq. Ft. — First Floor
1,094 Sq. Ft. — Second Floor
50,256 Cu. Ft.

Wherever built - north, east, south, or west - this home will surely command all the attention it deserves. And little wonder with such a well-designed exterior and such an outstanding interior. List your favorite features.

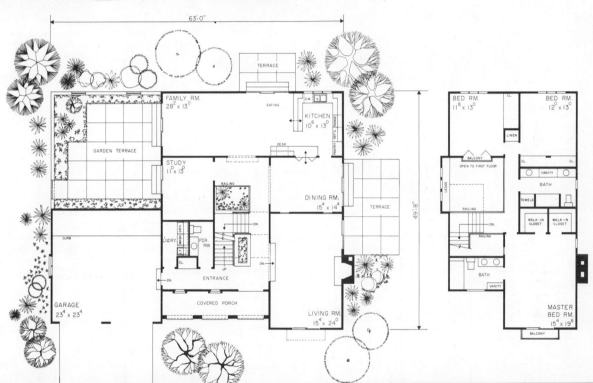

Design S 2512

2,074 Sq. Ft. — First Floor
1,116 Sq. Ft. — Second Floor
41,500 Cu. Ft.

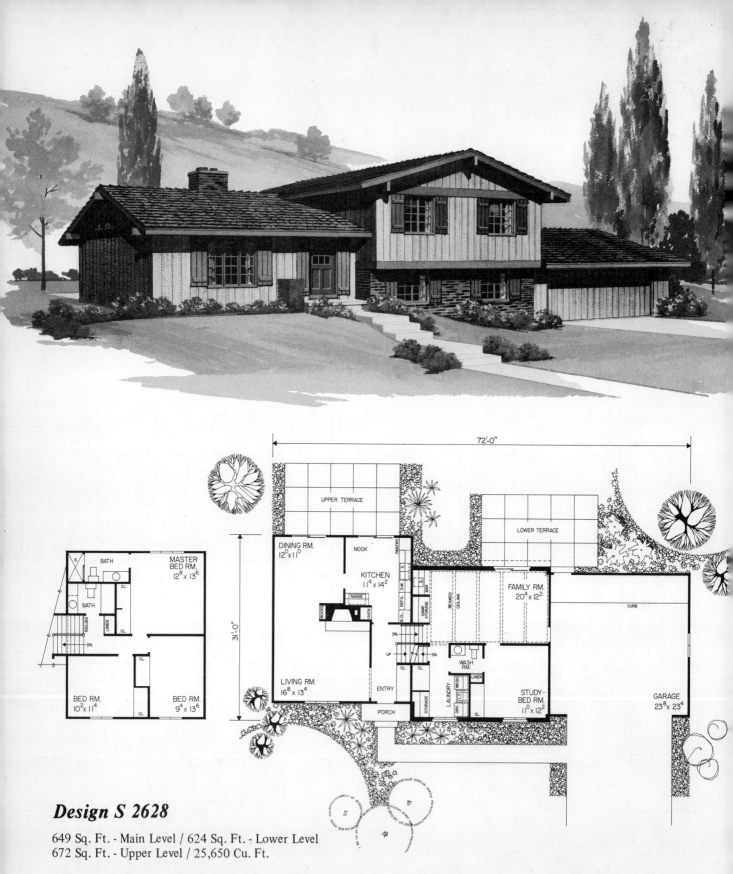

Design S 2628

649 Sq. Ft. - Main Level / 624 Sq. Ft. - Lower Level
672 Sq. Ft. - Upper Level / 25,650 Cu. Ft.

This Western home on the range has a rugged appeal all its own. Whatever its surroundings, its appeal will surely not go unnoticed. The low-pitched, wide-overhanging roofs play their part as effective sun visors during the hot summer months. Then, notice how the upper level provides protection for the lower level. Inside, there is four bedroom livability. While the upper level features three bedrooms and two baths, the lower level is where the fourth bedroom can be found. If you wish, make it a study or a guest room. Or even a home office. The extra wash room is nearby. The in-line kitchen features informal eating space, while the formal dining area is but a few steps away. A favorite spot will be the family room with its beamed ceiling. Don't miss laundry or stairs to basement level.

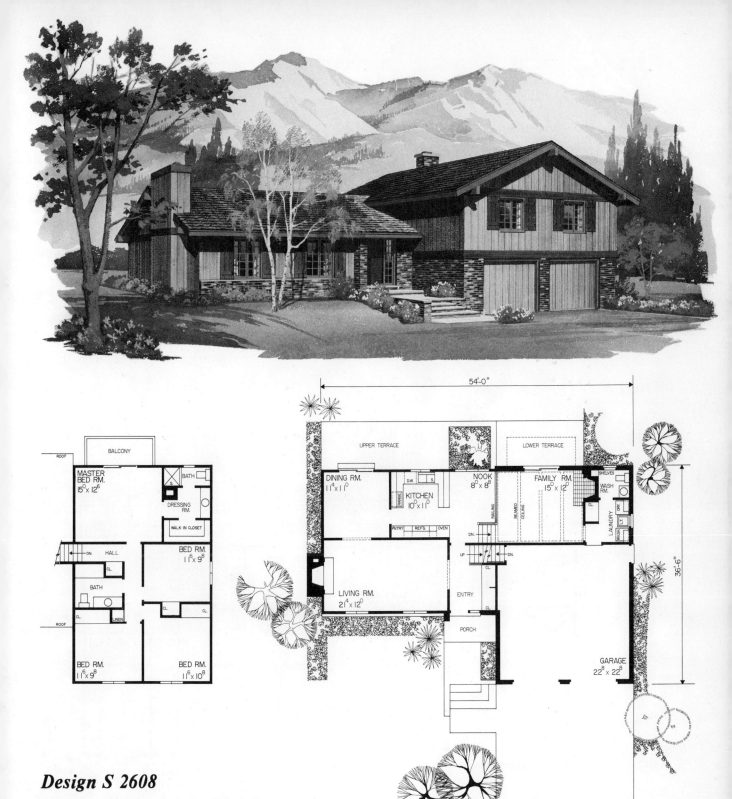

Design S 2608

728 Sq. Ft. - Main Level / 310 Sq. Ft. - Lower Level
874 Sq. Ft. - Upper Level / 27,705 Cu. Ft.

Once again, low-pitched wide-overhanging roofs set the character of an appealing, Western tri-level adaptation. The exposed rafter tails, vertical siding, board shutters and accent of brick further enhances the exterior attractiveness. This efficiently planned interior will deliver loads of livability for the money invested. The upper level, with four bedrooms and two full baths, means that the house will serve its occupants well for many years as the children grow up. Then, there is the invaluable feature of living and dining flexibility. The main level living room is spacious, has a fireplace and is free of unnecessary crossroom traffic. The lower level family room has a fireplace, too, and will provide that informal, multi-purpose living area. A beamed ceiling adds to the atmosphere. The fine-functioning kitchen is flanked by the formal dining room and the breakfast nook. For outdoor enjoyment there is the upper level balcony and the lower terraces.

Design S 2231   2,740 Sq. Ft./31,670 Cu. Ft.

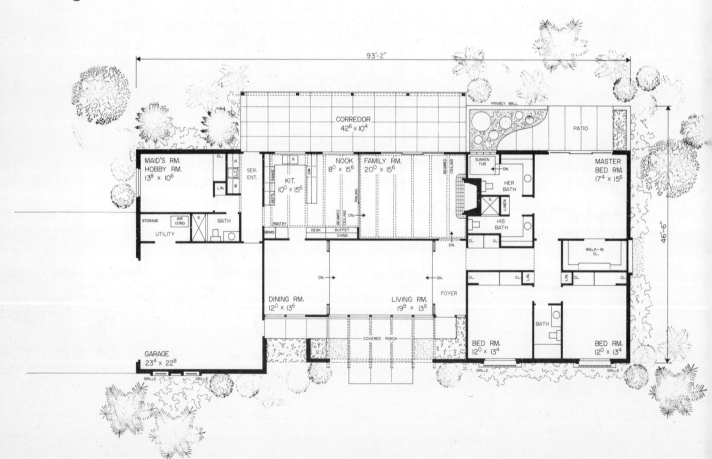

The features that will appeal to you about this flat-roofed Spanish hacienda are almost endless. Of course, the captivating qualities of the exterior speak for themselves. The extension of the front bedroom wall to form the inviting arch is distinctive. Once inside, any list of features will continue to grow rapidly. Notice "her" and "his" baths. One bath has a sunken tub, the other a stall shower. Each has a built-in vanity top. A second bath conveniently services the children's rooms. Storage in this area is excellent. Both the family and living rooms are sunken. The kitchen is efficient with pantry, desk and china/buffet nearby. Around the corner is the service entrance. Note hobby room third bath, and rear corredor. Also, private patio.

Design S 2386   1,994 Sq. Ft./22,160 Cu. Ft.

This distinctive home may look like the Far West, but don't let that inhibit you from enjoying the great livability it has to offer. Wherever built, you will surely experience a satisfying pride of ownership. Imagine, an entrance court in addition to a large side courtyard! A central core is made up of the living, dining, and family rooms, plus the kitchen. Each functions with an outdoor living area. The younger generation has its sleeping zone divorced from the master bedroom. The location of the attractive attached garage provides direct access to the front entry. Don't miss the vanity, the utility room with laundry equipment, the snack bar, and the raised hearth fireplace. Note three pass-throughs from kitchen. Observe the beamed and sloping ceiling.

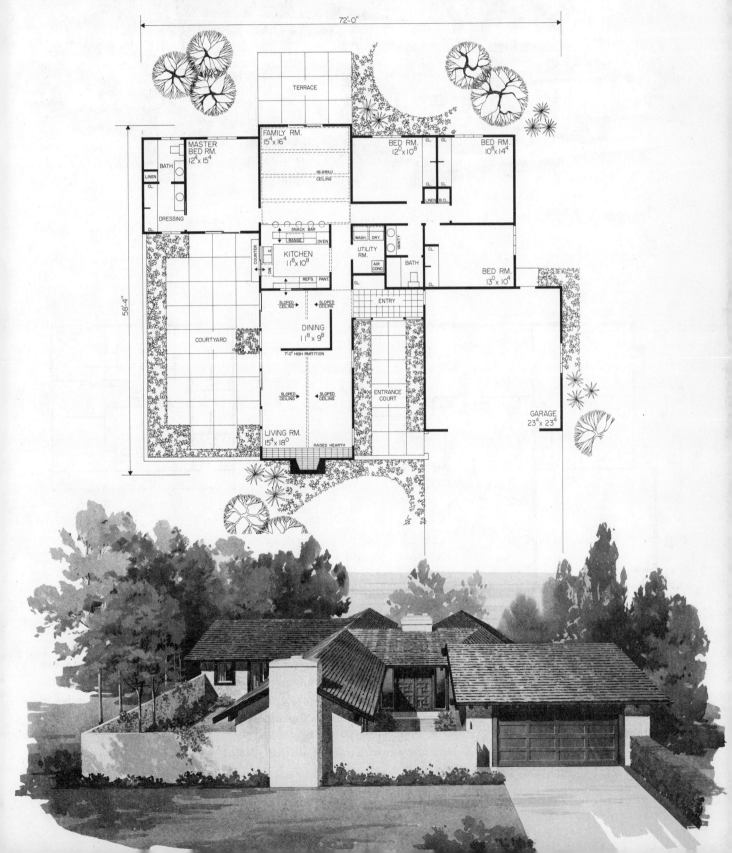

Design S 1753 1,580 Sq. Ft. — First Floor / 1,008 Sq. Ft. — Second Floor / 26,484 Cu. Ft.

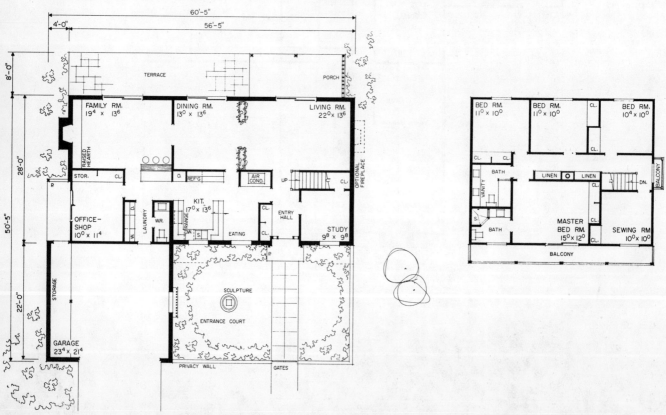

The charm of the old Spanish Southwest is captured by the rugged individualism characterized by this design. If a large and growing family demanded, this design could function wonderfully as a five bedroom home. In addition to this great potential, there is all that livability downstairs. The family, dining and living rooms will cater to the family's informal and formal group activities most adequately. But then, should a member wish to be alone with his reading or hobby there are two first floor rooms waiting to serve the study and shop. If necessary, either of these two rooms could function as a home office. This non-basement home has separate laundry, wash room.

Design S 2214

3,011 Sq. Ft. — First Floor
2,297 Sq. Ft. — Second Floor
78,585 Cu. Ft.

A Spanish hacienda with all the appeal and all the comforts one would want in a new home. This is a house that looks big and really is big. Measuring 100 feet across the front with various appendages and roof planes, this design gives the appearance of a cluster of units. And with the long balcony and overhanging roof the size appears even greater. The house represents over 5,000 square feet without the garage. And the available living space is utilized in grand fashion. There are five bedrooms on the second floor plus a sixth and a study on the first. The master bedroom features two full baths and a sleeping porch. The living room is 27 feet long and if you wanted more space you could do away with the plant area. Or, maybe you'd prefer to make this a music area. The 18 foot dining room will seat a house full. The kitchen is nearby, but a step from the breakfast nook and the family room. Then there is the three car garage with a big bulk storage room. Don't overlook the private front courtyard. Just a great house for the large, active family.

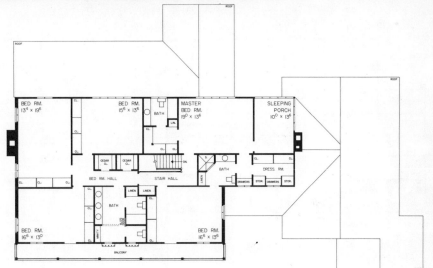

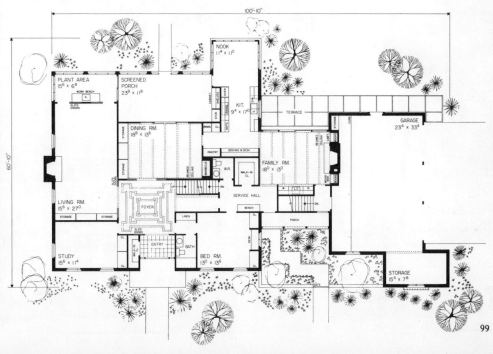

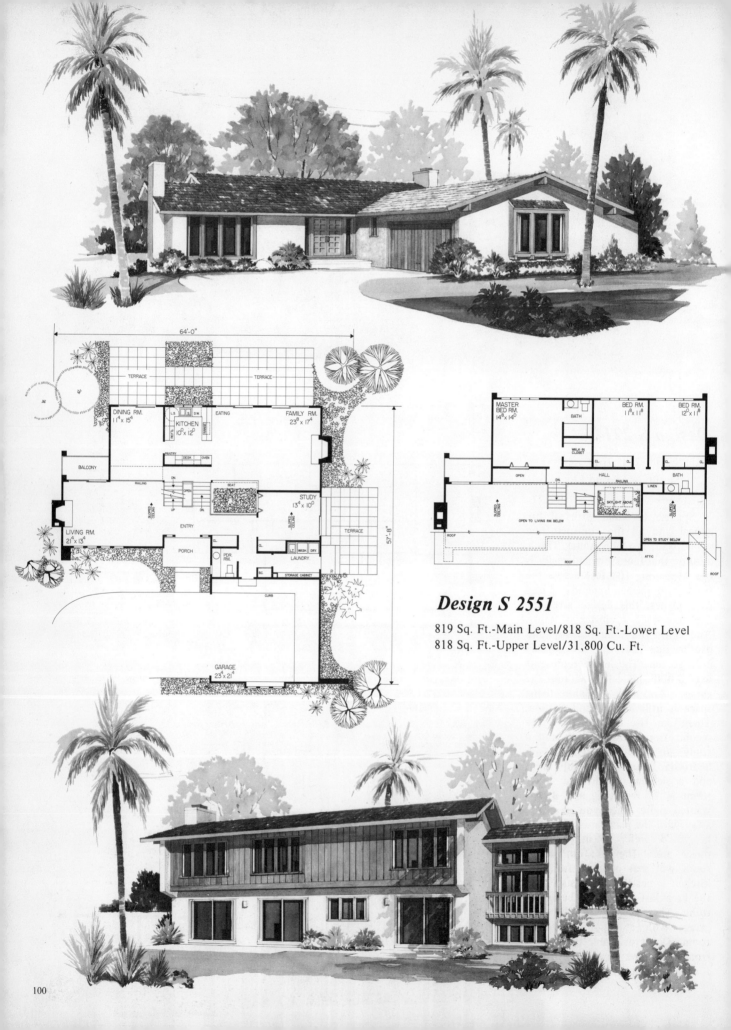

Floor Plan Labels

Main Level (left floor plan):

64'-0"

TERRACE TERRACE

DINING RM.
11⁴ x 15⁴

KITCHEN
10⁰ x 12²

EATING

FAMILY RM.
23⁸ x 17⁴

BALCONY

PANTRY DESK OVEN

RAILING

SEAT

STUDY
13⁸ x 10⁰

TERRACE

57'-8"

LIVING RM.
21⁴ x 13⁴

ENTRY

PORCH

PDR. RM.

LAUNDRY

STORAGE CABINET

CURB

GARAGE
23⁴ x 21⁴

Upper Level (right floor plan):

MASTER BED RM.
14⁸ x 14⁰

BATH

BED RM.
11⁸ x 11⁸

BED RM.
12⁰ x 11⁰

WALK IN CLOSET

OPEN

HALL

RAILING

LINEN

BATH

SLOPED CEILING

OPEN TO LIVING RM. BELOW

SKYLIGHT ABOVE

SLOPED CEILING

ROOF

OPEN TO STUDY BELOW

ROOF

ATTIC

ROOF

Design S 2551

819 Sq. Ft.-Main Level/818 Sq. Ft.-Lower Level
818 Sq. Ft.-Upper Level/31,800 Cu. Ft.

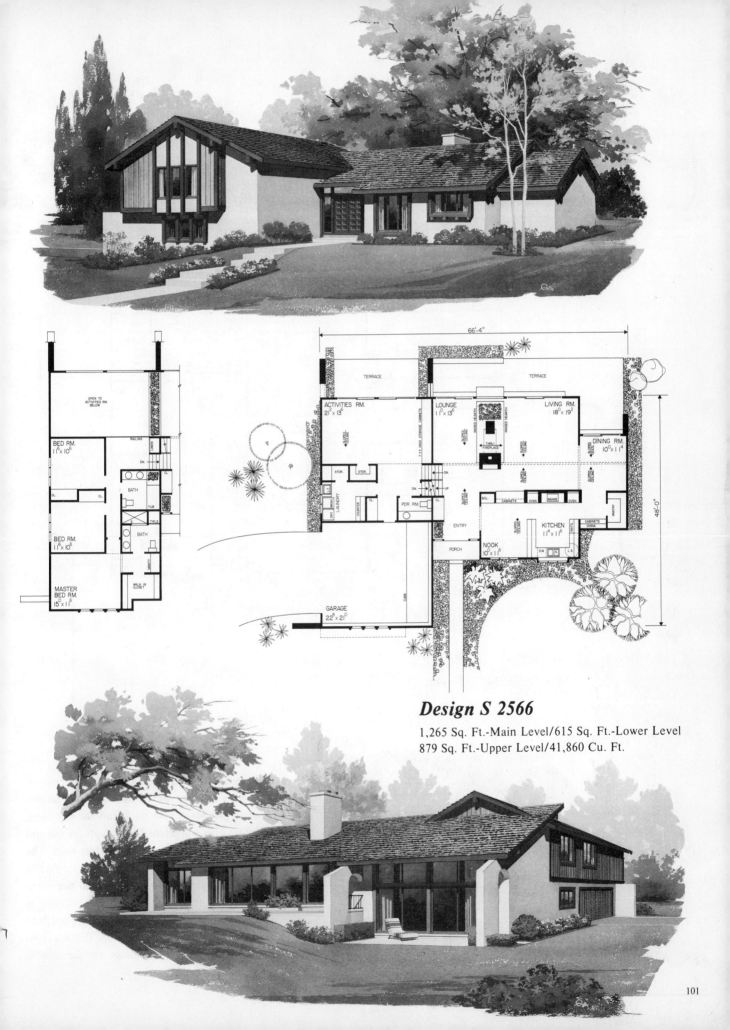

Design S 2566

1,265 Sq. Ft.-Main Level/615 Sq. Ft.-Lower Level
879 Sq. Ft.-Upper Level/41,860 Cu. Ft.

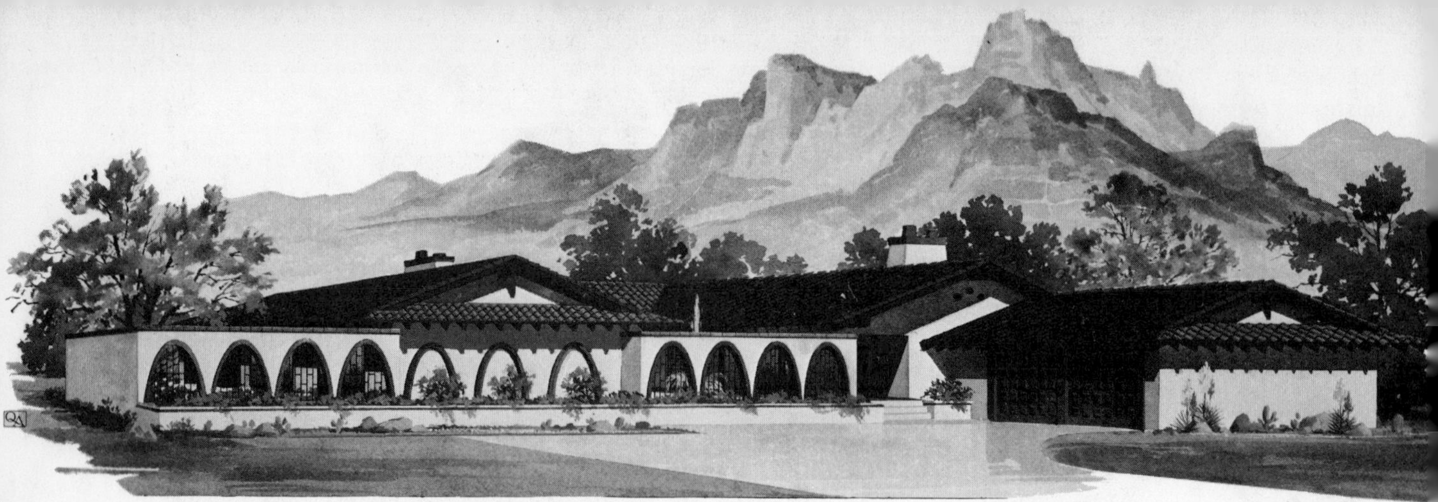

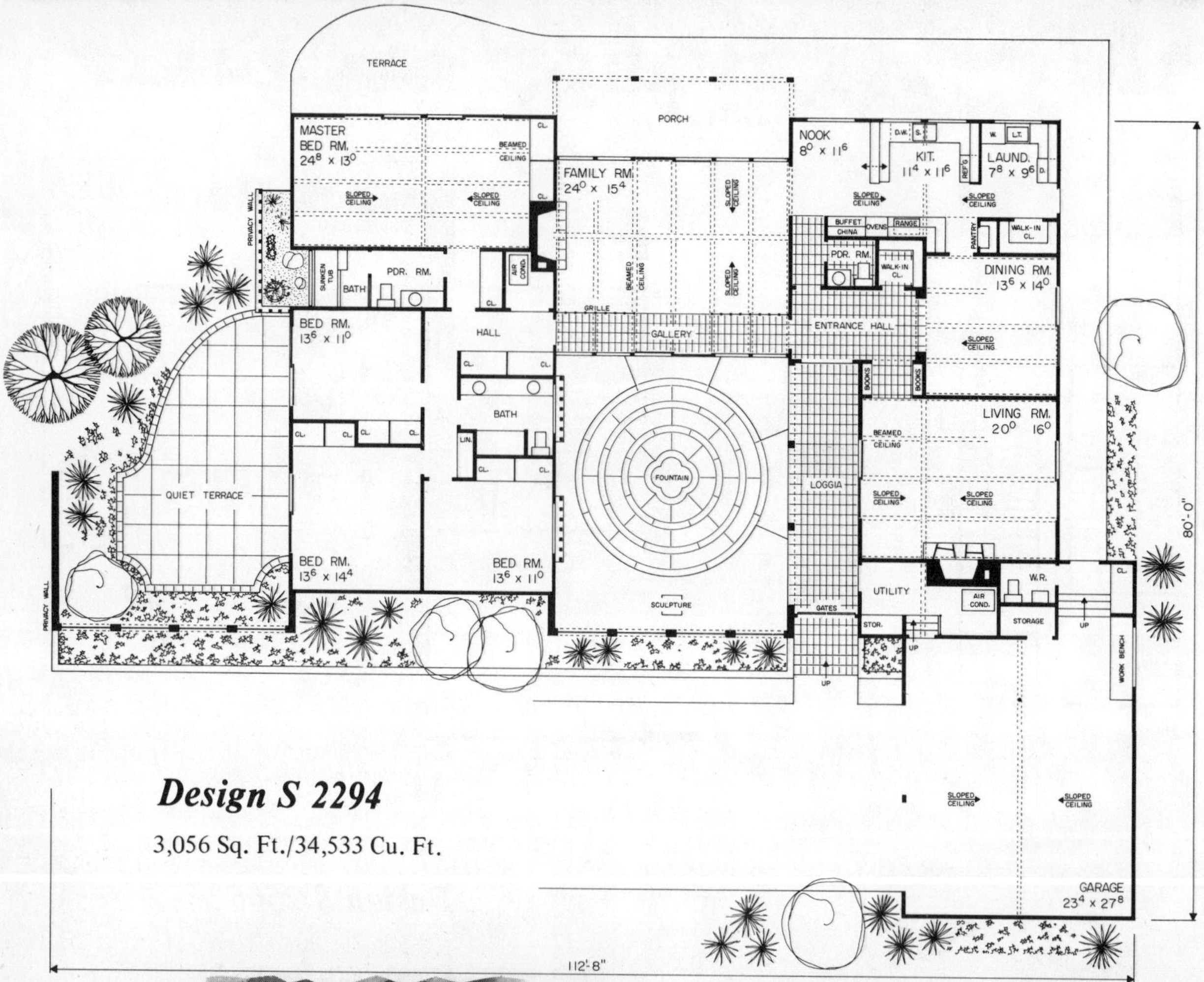

TERRACE
PORCH
MASTER BED RM. $24^{8} \times 13^{0}$
BEAMED CEILING
SLOPED CEILING
FAMILY RM. $24^{0} \times 15^{4}$
NOOK $8^{0} \times 11^{6}$
KIT. $11^{4} \times 11^{6}$
LAUND. $7^{8} \times 9^{6}$
PRIVACY WALL
SUNKEN TUB
BATH
PDR. RM.
AIR COND.
BUFFET CHINA
OVENS
RANGE
PANTRY
WALK-IN CL.
DINING RM. $13^{6} \times 14^{0}$
BED RM. $13^{6} \times 11^{0}$
HALL
GRILLE
GALLERY
ENTRANCE HALL
BOOKS
LIVING RM. $20^{0} \times 16^{0}$
QUIET TERRACE
FOUNTAIN
LOGGIA
BED RM. $13^{6} \times 14^{4}$
BED RM. $13^{6} \times 11^{0}$
SCULPTURE
GATES
UTILITY
STOR.
W.R.
STORAGE
UP
WORK BENCH
GARAGE $23^{4} \times 27^{8}$
80'-0"
112'-8"

Design S 2294

3,056 Sq. Ft./34,533 Cu. Ft.

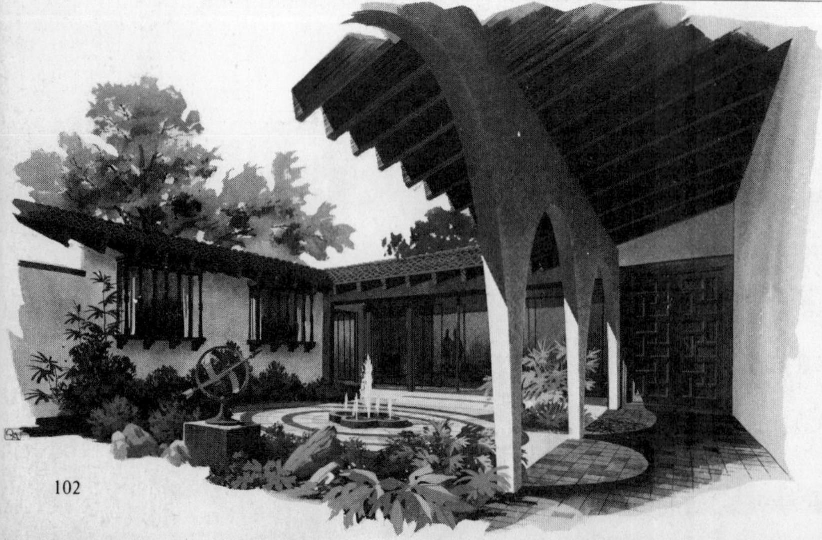

Here is a western ranch with an authentic Spanish flavor. Striking a note of distinction, the arched privacy walls provide a fine backdrop for the long, raised planter. The low-pitched roof features tile and has a wide overhang with exposed rafter tails. The interior is wonderfully zoned. The all-purpose family room is flanked by the sleeping wing and the living wing. Study each area carefully for the planning is excellent and the features are many. Indoor-outdoor integration is outstanding. At left – the spacious interior court. The covered passage to the double front doors is dramatic, indeed.

Echoing design themes of old Spain, this history house distills the essence of country houses built by rancheros in Early California. Yet its floor plan provides all the comfort and convenience essential to contemporary living. A-mong its charming features are a se-cluded court, or patio; a greenhouse tucked in behind the garage; a covered rear porch; a low-pitched wide over-hanging roof with exposed rafter tails; sloping beamed ceilings. Contributing to the authenticity of the design are the two sets of panelled doors. The covered walk to the front doors pro-vides a sheltered area adjacent to the court. Once inside, the feeling of space continues to impress.

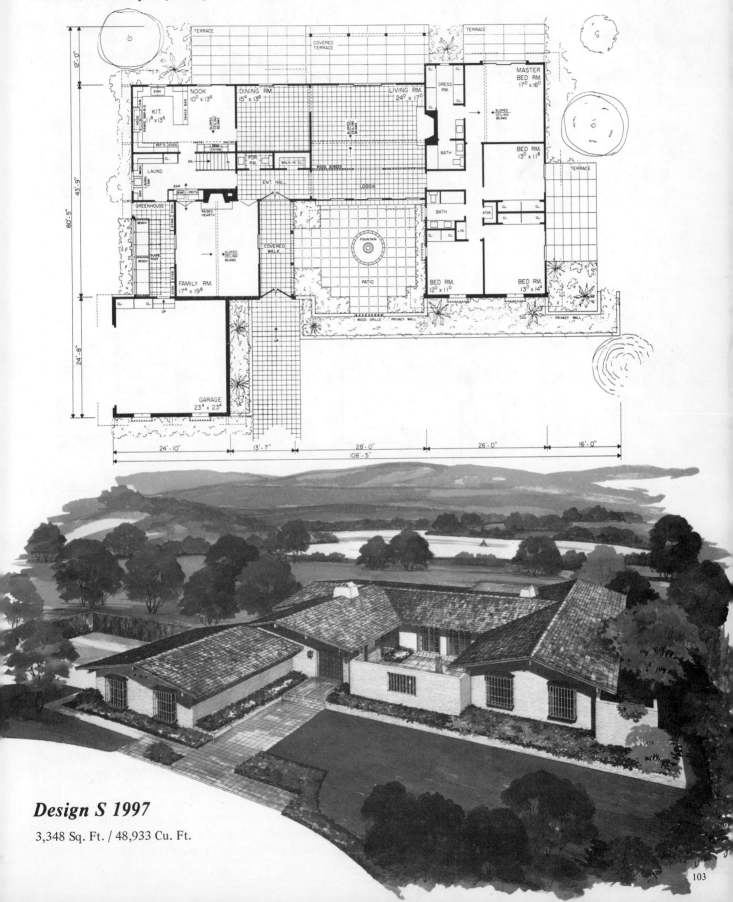

Design S 1997

3,348 Sq. Ft. / 48,933 Cu. Ft.

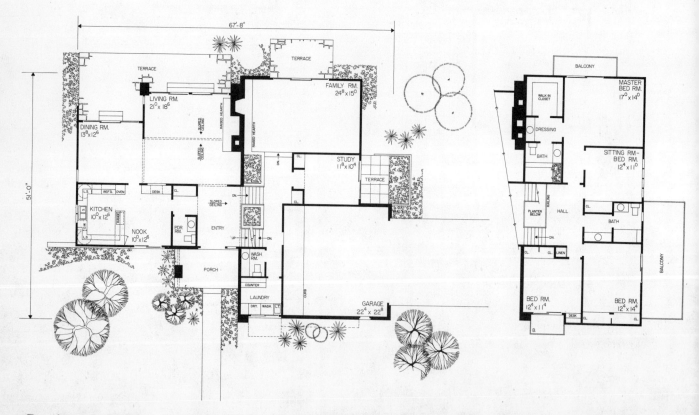

Design S 2536
1,077 Sq. Ft.-Main Level/1,319 Sq. Ft.-Upper Level/914 Sq. Ft.-Lower Level/31,266 Cu. Ft.

Here are three levels of outstanding liv-ability all packed in a delightfully contemporary exterior. The low pitch-ed roof has a wide overhang with ex-posed rafter tails. The stone masses contrast effectively with the vertical siding and the glass areas. The exten-sion of the sloping roof provides the recessed feature of the front entrance with the patterned double doors. The homemaker's favorite highlight will be the layout of the kitchen. No cross-room traffic here. Only a few steps from the formal and informal eating areas, it is the epitome of effiency. A sloping beamed ceiling, sliding glass doors, and a raised hearth fireplace en-hance the appeal of the living room. The upper level offers the option of a fourth bedroom or a sitting room func-tioning with the master bedroom. Note the three balconies. On the lower level, the big family room, quiet study, laun-dry, extra washroom.

The Refreshing Attraction of **Contemporary Houses**

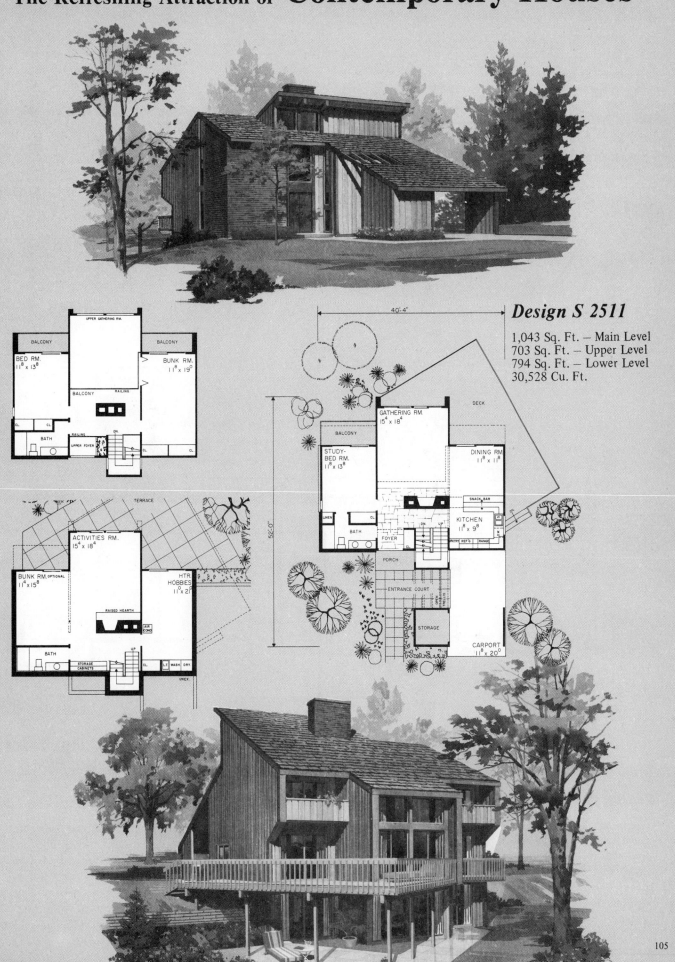

Design S 2511

1,043 Sq. Ft. — Main Level
703 Sq. Ft. — Upper Level
794 Sq. Ft. — Lower Level
30,528 Cu. Ft.

Upper Level:
UPPER GATHERING RM.
BALCONY
BALCONY
BED RM. 11⁸ x 13⁸
BUNK RM. 11⁸ x 19⁰
BALCONY
RAILING
CL. CL.
BATH
RAILING
UPPER FOYER
DN.
CL. CL.

Main Level:
40'-4"
52'-0"
DECK
GATHERING RM. 15⁴ x 18⁴
BALCONY
STUDY-BED RM. 11⁸ x 13⁸
DINING RM. 11⁸ x 11⁸
SNACK BAR
KITCHEN 11⁸ x 9⁸
LINEN
BATH
CL
FOYER
DN. UP
PANTRY REF'G RANGE
CL
PORCH
ENTRANCE COURT
OPEN BRICK TRELLIS
STORAGE
CARPORT 11⁸ x 20⁰

Lower Level:
TERRACE
ACTIVITIES RM. 15⁴ x 18⁴
BUNK RM. OPTIONAL 11⁴ x 15⁸
HTR. HOBBIES 11⁰ x 21⁰
RAISED HEARTH
AIR COND.
BATH
STORAGE CABINETS
UP
CL.
LT WASH DRY
UNEX.

105

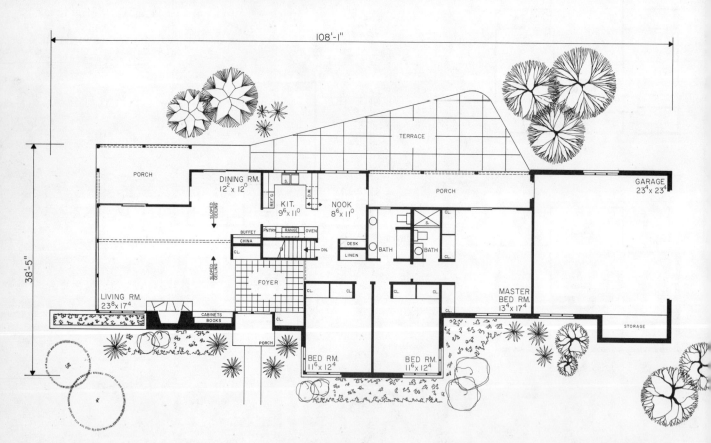

Design S 2330   1,854 Sq. Ft. / 30,001 Cu. Ft.

Your family will never tire of the living patterns offered by this appealing home with its low-pitched, wide overhanging roof. The masonry masses of the exterior are pleasing. While the blueprints call for the use of stone, you may wish to substitute brick veneer. Sloping ceiling and plenty of glass will assure the living area of a fine feeling of spaciousness. Two covered porches enhance the enjoyment of outdoor living. Two baths serve the three bedroom sleeping area. Not to be overlooked are such features as the fireplace wall, the built-ins, the basement for extra recreational space, and the large garage with its storage area. The kitchen overlooking the rear yard is strategically located between dining room and nook. A sound investment for these years of high inflation.

Design S 2534

3,262 Sq. Ft./58,640 Cu. Ft.

The angular wings of this ranch home surely contribute to the unique character of the exterior. These wings effectively balance what is truly a dramatic and inviting front entrance. Massive masonry walls support the wide overhanging roof with its exposed wood beams. The patterned double front doors are surrounded by delightful expanses of glass. The raised planters and the masses of quarried stone (make it brick if you prefer) enhance the exterior appeal. Inside, a distinctive and practical floor plan stands ready to shape and serve the living patterns of the active family. The spacious entrance hall highlights sloped ceiling and an attractive open stairway to the lower level recreation area. An impressive fireplace and an abundance of glass are features of the big gathering room. Interestingly shaped dining room and study flank this main living area. The large kitchen offers many of the charming aspects of the family-kitchen of yesteryear. The bedroom wing offers a sunken master bedroom suite.

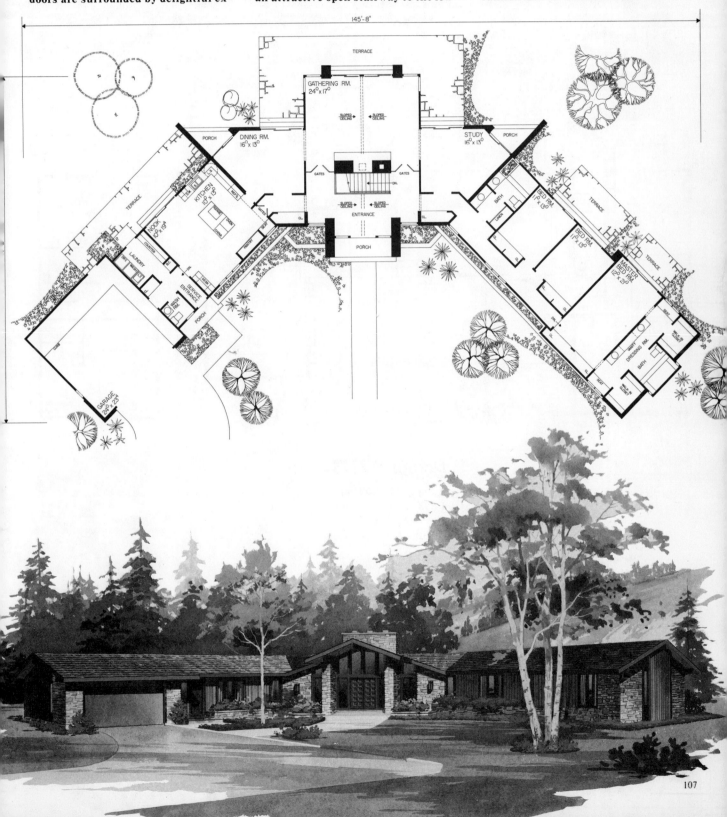

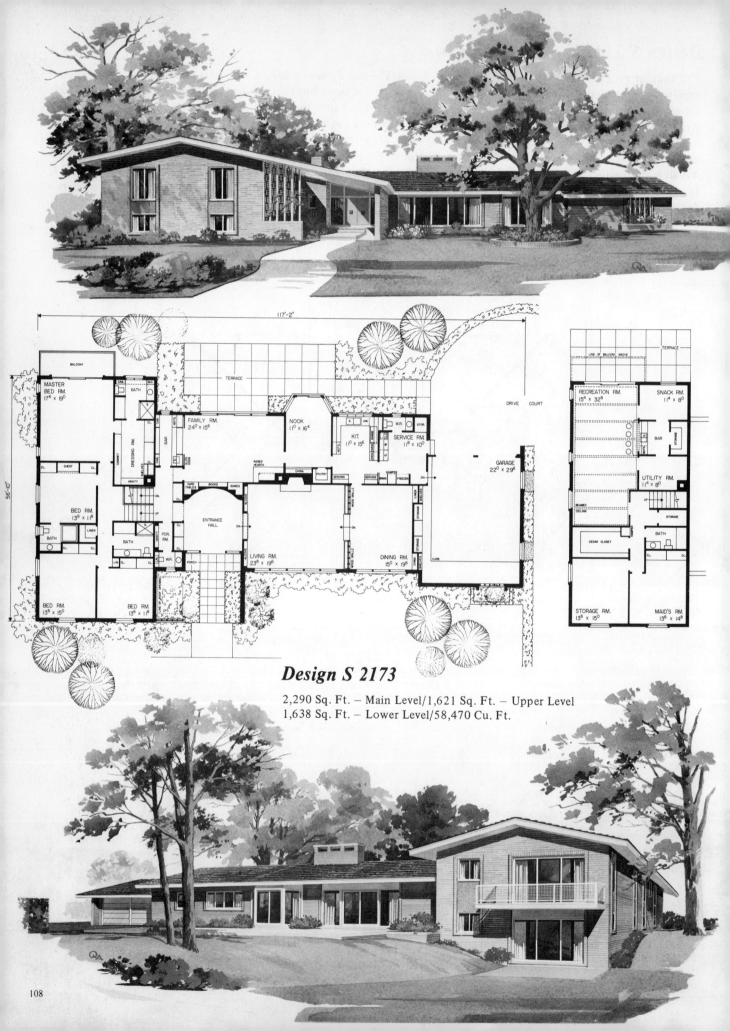

Design S 2173

2,290 Sq. Ft. – Main Level/1,621 Sq. Ft. – Upper Level
1,638 Sq. Ft. – Lower Level/58,470 Cu. Ft.

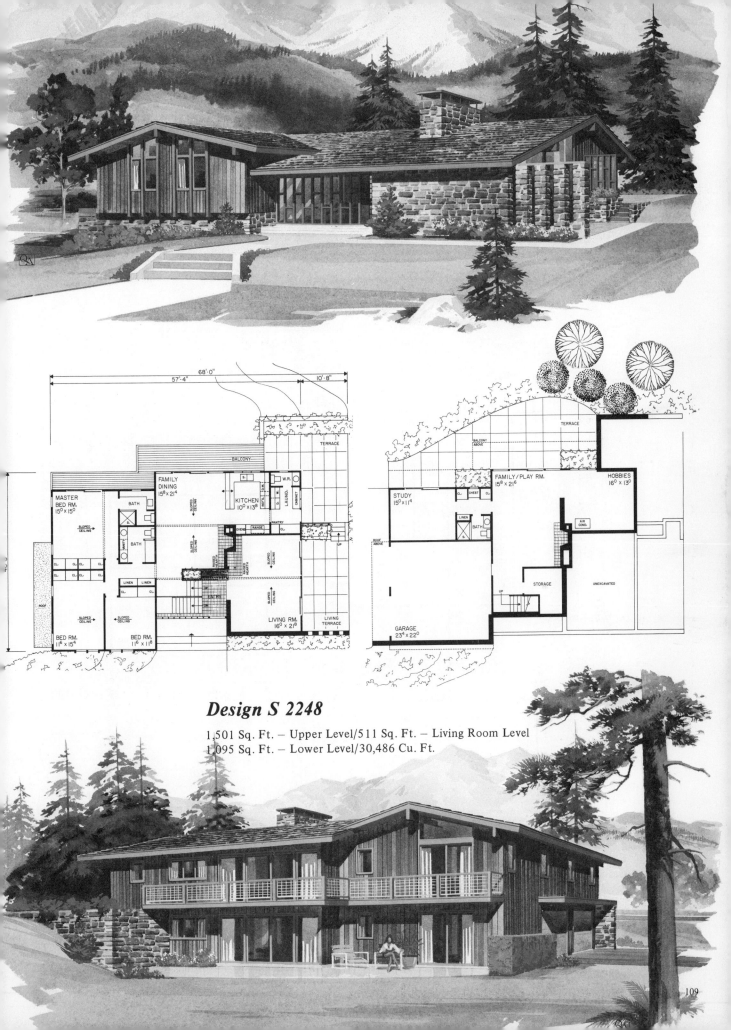

Design S 2248

1,501 Sq. Ft. — Upper Level/511 Sq. Ft. — Living Room Level
1,095 Sq. Ft. — Lower Level/30,486 Cu. Ft.

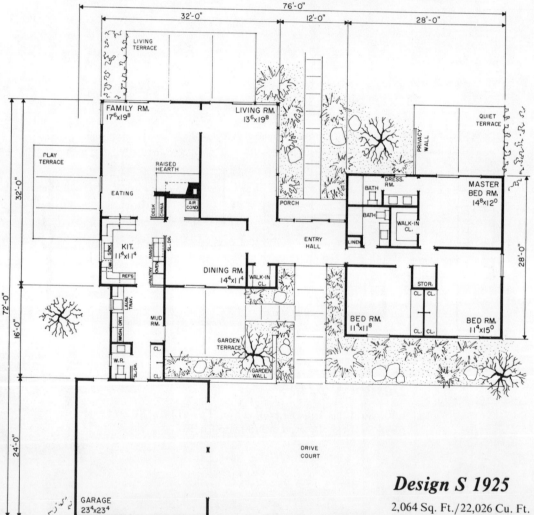

Design S 1925

2,064 Sq. Ft./22,026 Cu. Ft.

New and refreshing living patterns can take many forms. Here, living patterns are related in such a manner as to result in what appears to be three distinct units, attached by passageways to produce a "cluster". If ever you've wished that your sleeping area could enjoy complete privacy from the rest of the house, you should find this unique plan of interest. If ever you wished you could take only a couple of steps in one direction and be in the dining room, and a couple in another direction and be in the family room, this practical plan will appeal to you. And, if you ever wished you could really control the entry of dirt and mud you'll appreciate this plan.

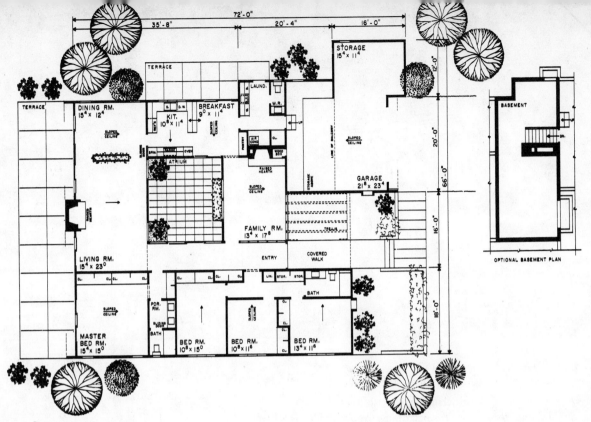

Design S 2135

2,490 Sq. Ft.-Excluding Atrium/28,928 Cu. Ft.

For those seeking a new experience in home ownership. The proud occupants of this contemporary home will forever be thrilled at their choice of such a distinguished exterior and such a practical and exciting floor plan.

The variety of shed roof planes contrast dramatically with the simplicity of the vertical siding. Inside there is a feeling of spaciousness resulting from the sloping ceilings. The uniqueness of this design is further enhanced by

the atrium. Open to the sky, this outdoor area, indoors, can be enjoyed from all parts of the house. The sleeping zone has four bedrooms, two baths, and plenty of closets. The informal living zone has a fine kitchen, breakfast room.

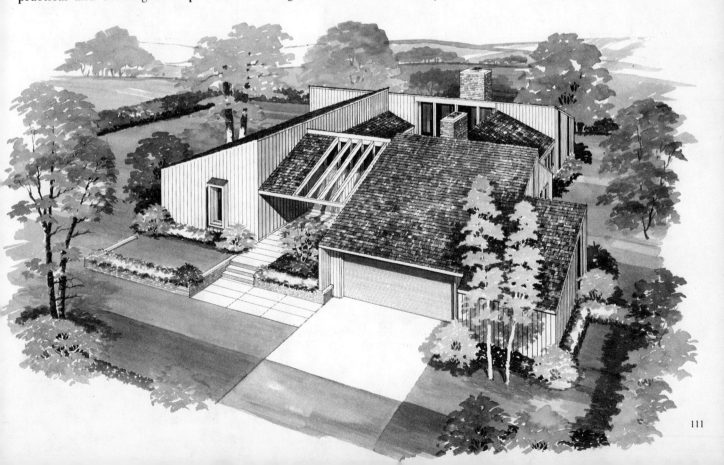

Design S 2581
2,125 Sq. Ft. – First Floor
903 Sq. Ft. – Second Floor / 54,476 Cu. Ft.

A study with a fireplace! A gathering room with a sloped ceiling and adjoining terrace. A formal dining room and screened-in porch. A balcony lounge. A kitchen with built-ins. Plus a separate breakfast nook. Lots of extras here!

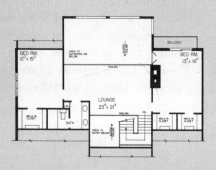

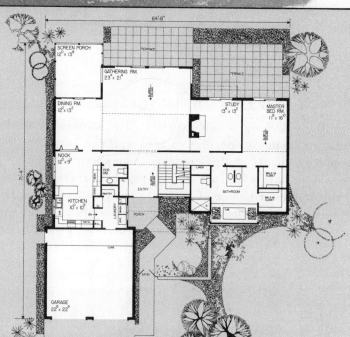

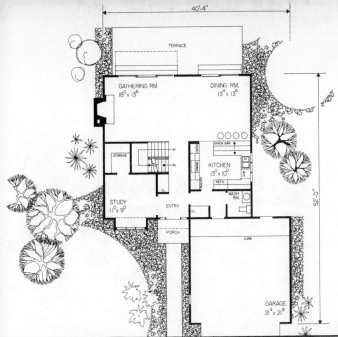

Design S 2711
975 Sq. Ft. — First Floor
1,024 Sq. Ft. — Second Floor / 31,380 Cu. Ft.

Special features! A complete master suite with a private balcony. A study. A convenient bar. Plus a gathering room, and dining room that measure 31' wide.

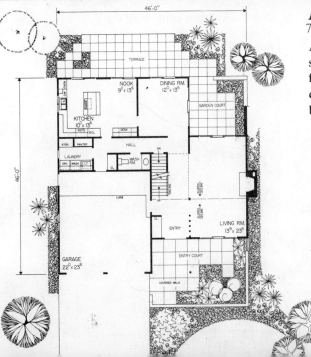

Design S 2582
1,195 Sq. Ft. — First Floor
731 Sq. Ft. — Second Floor / 32,500 Cu. Ft.

An enclosed courtyard welcomes guests to this home! Inside, the living room opens onto another garden court. And features a sloped ceiling and traditional fireplace. A formal dining room. And a kitchen with built-ins plus a cheerful breakfast nook that opens onto the terrace.

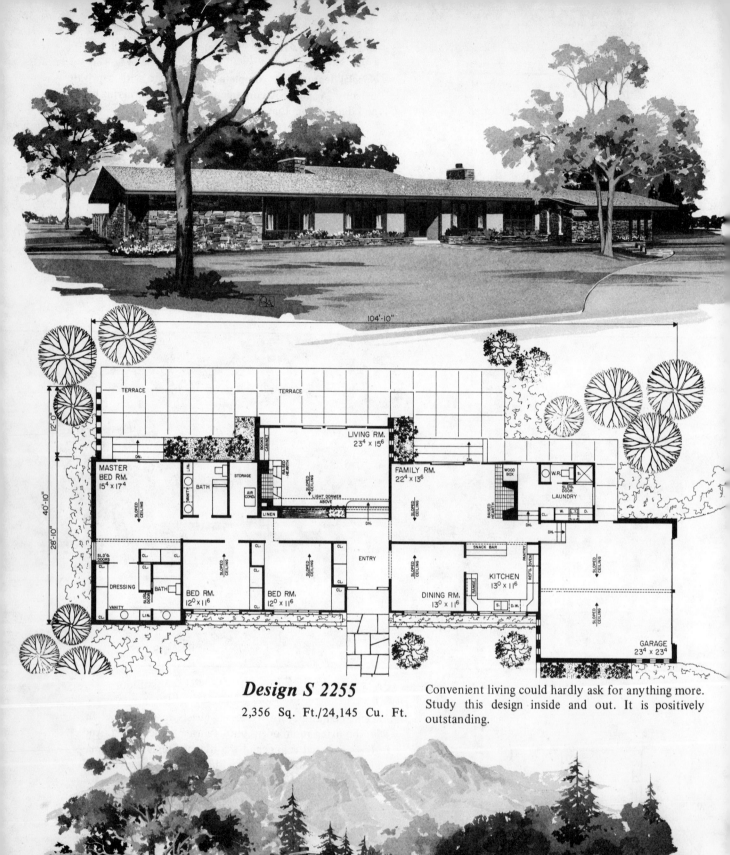

Design S 2255

2,356 Sq. Ft./24,145 Cu. Ft.

Convenient living could hardly ask for anything more. Study this design inside and out. It is positively outstanding.

MASTER BED RM. 15⁴ x 17⁴

LIVING RM. 23⁴ x 15⁶

FAMILY RM. 22⁴ x 13⁶

LAUNDRY

DRESSING

BED RM. 12⁰ x 11⁶

BED RM. 12⁰ x 11⁶

ENTRY

DINING RM. 13⁰ x 11⁶

KITCHEN 13⁰ x 11⁶

GARAGE 23⁴ x 23⁴

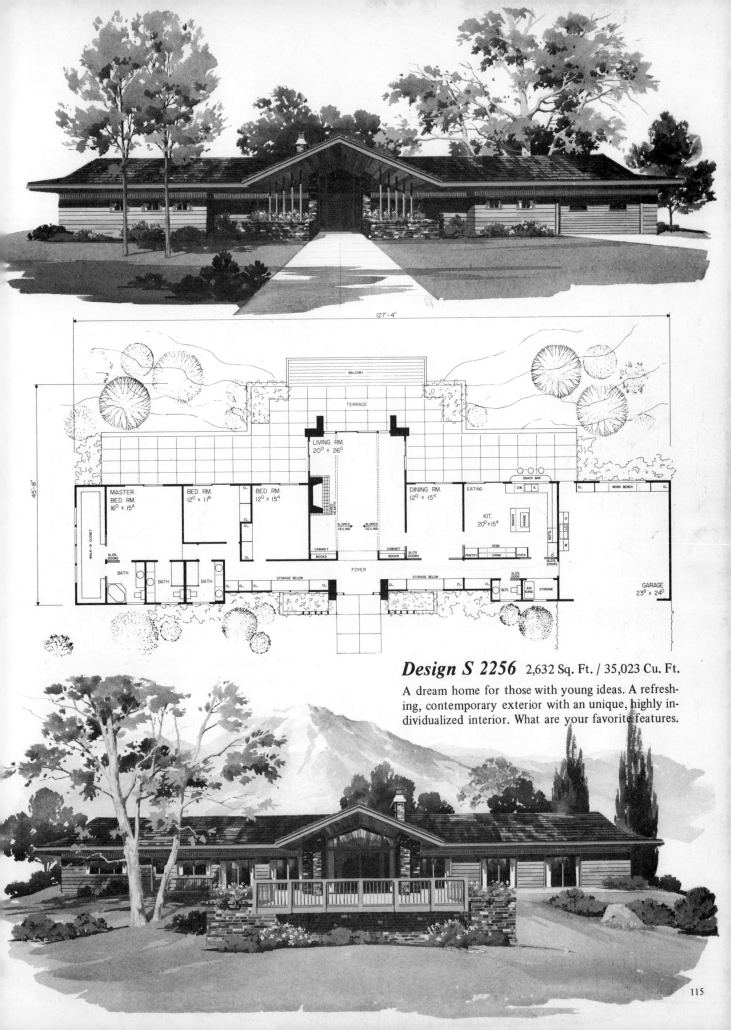

Design S 2256 2,632 Sq. Ft. / 35,023 Cu. Ft.

A dream home for those with young ideas. A refreshing, contemporary exterior with an unique, highly individualized interior. What are your favorite features.

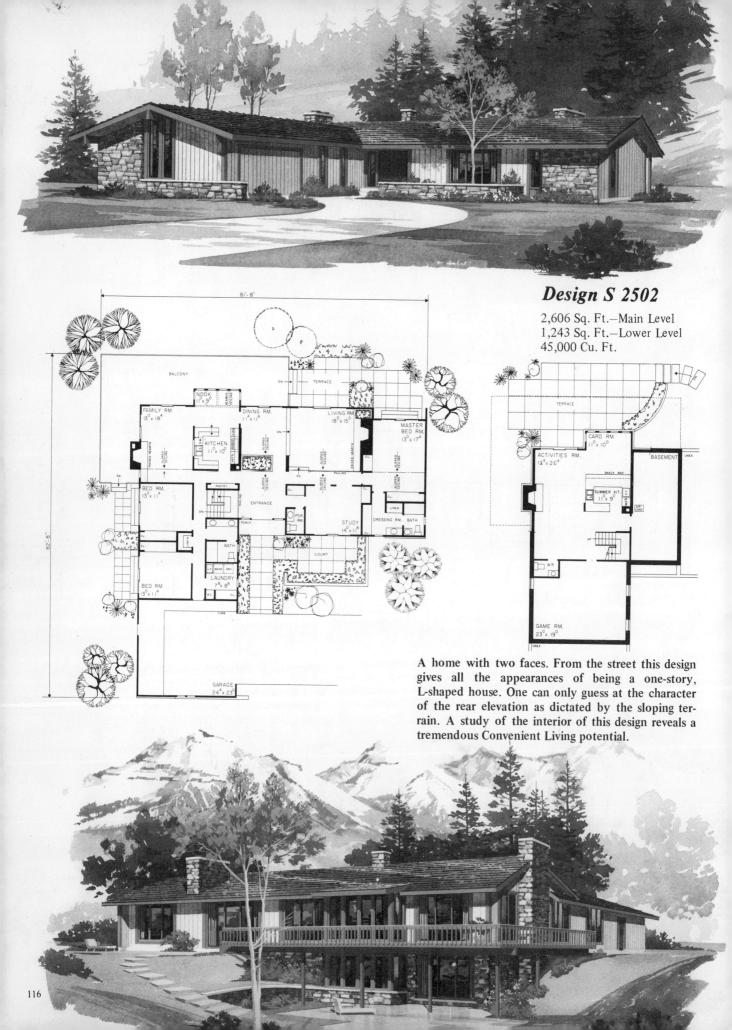

Design S 2502

2,606 Sq. Ft.—Main Level
1,243 Sq. Ft.—Lower Level
45,000 Cu. Ft.

A home with two faces. From the street this design gives all the appearances of being a one-story, L-shaped house. One can only guess at the character of the rear elevation as dictated by the sloping terrain. A study of the interior of this design reveals a tremendous Convenient Living potential.

Design S 2504

1,918 Sq. Ft. – Main Level
1,910 Sq. Ft. – Lower Level
39,800 Cu. Ft.

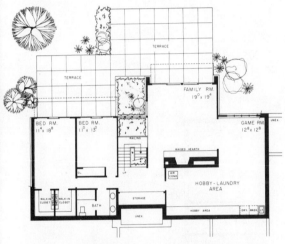

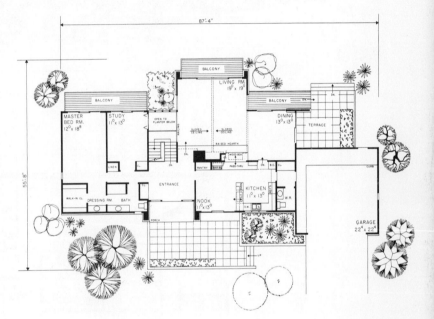

Taking advantage of that sloping site can result in the opening up of a lower level which can double the available living area. Such has been the case in this hillside design. Study the interior carefully. This design offers tremendous living potential to the active family.

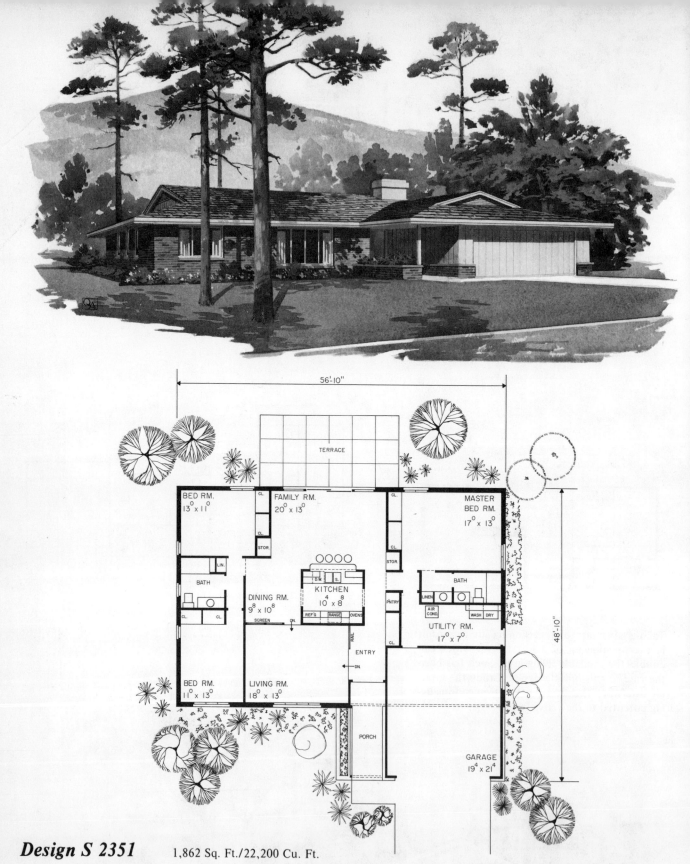

TERRACE

BED RM.
13⁰ x 11⁰

FAMILY RM.
20⁰ x 13⁰

CL.

CL.

STOR.

MASTER
BED RM.
17⁰ x 13⁰

CL.

LIN.

BATH

STOR.

CL.

BATH

LINEN

AIR
COND.

WASH DRY

CL.

CL.

DINING RM.
9⁸ x 10⁸

KITCHEN
10 x 8

D.W. S.

REF'G RANGE OVENS

PNTRY

UTILITY RM.
17⁰ x 7⁰

SCREEN   DN

RAIL

BED RM.
11⁰ x 13⁰

LIVING RM.
18⁰ x 13⁰

ENTRY

DN.

CL.

PORCH

GARAGE
19⁴ x 21⁴

56'-10"

48'-10"

Design S 2351   1,862 Sq. Ft./22,200 Cu. Ft.

The extension of the wide overhanging roof of this distinctive home provides shelter for the walkway to the front door. A raised brick planter adds appeal. The living patterns offered by this plan are delightfully different, yet extremely practical. Notice the separation of the master bedroom from the other two bedrooms. While assuring an extra measure of quiet privacy for the parents, this master bedroom location may be ideal for a live-in-relative. Locating the kitchen in the middle of the plan frees up valuable outside wall space and leads to interesting planning. Observe its proximity to all areas. The front dining room is sunken for dramatic appeal and need not have any crossroom traffic. The utility room houses the laundry and the heating and the cooling equipment.

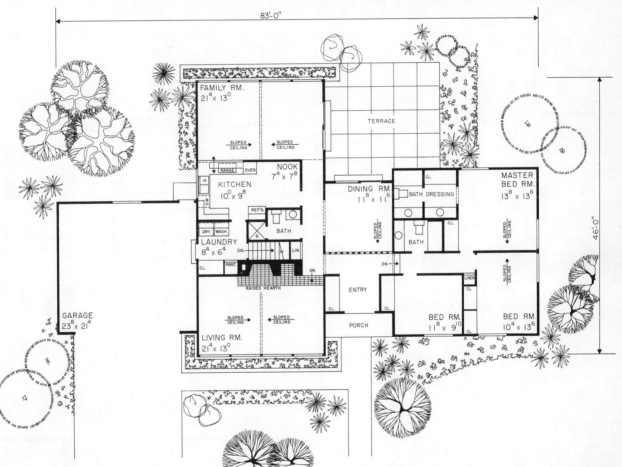

Design S 2363   1,978 Sq. Ft./27,150 Cu. Ft.

You will have a lot of fun deciding what you like best about this home with its eye-catching glass-gabled living room and wrap-around raised planter. A covered porch shelters the double front doors. Projecting to the rear is a family room identical in size with the

formal living room. Between these two rooms there are features galore. There is the efficient kitchen with pass-thru and informal eating space. Then there is the laundry with a closet, pantry, and the basement stairs nearby. Also, a full bath featuring a stall shower. The

dining room has a sloped ceiling and an appealing, open vertical divider which acts as screening from the entry. The three bedroom, two bath sleeping zone is sunken. Note the extra lavatory of the master bath. The raised hearth fireplace has an adjacent woodbox.

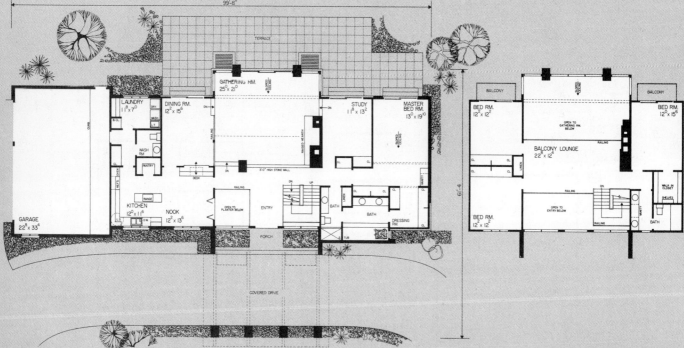

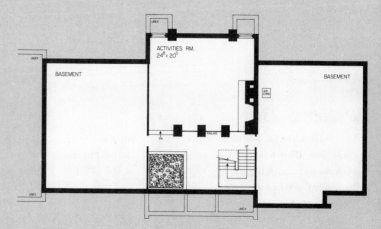

Design S 2562

2,884 Sq. Ft — Main Level / 864 Sq. Ft. — Upper Level
1,104 Sq. Ft — Lower Level / 73,625 Cu. Ft.

Four bedrooms! Including two with private balconies
and a master suite with a sloped ceiling. A balcony
lounge. Two fireplaces . . . one in the double-storied
gathering room, another in the activities room. A
study. A formal dining room. And a kitchen with a
dining nook, pantry and lots of built-ins. Soaring
lines and open space. Plus a design that allows privacy.
This is a home to suit any life style.

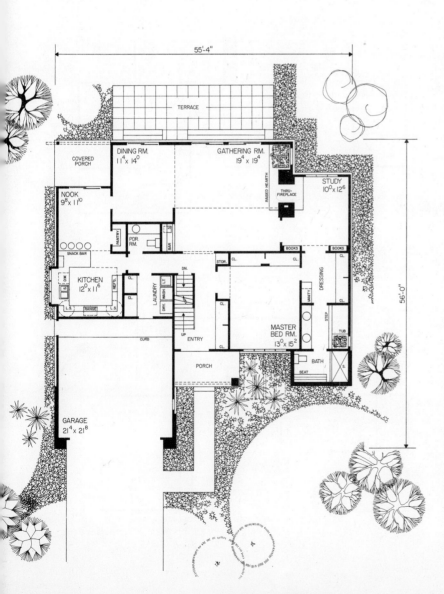

First Floor

TERRACE

55'-4"

DINING RM.
11'4 x 14'0

GATHERING RM.
19'4 x 19'4

COVERED PORCH

NOOK
9'8 x 11'10

STUDY
10'0 x 12'6

RAISED HEARTH

THRU-FIREPLACE

PANTRY

POR. RM.

BAR

SNACK BAR

BOOKS

BOOKS

STOR.

CL.

CL.

KITCHEN
12'0 x 11'6

REF.

LAUNDRY

WASH.

L.T.

DRY.

DN.

CL.

DRESSING

CL.

RANGE

CL.

UP ENTRY

CL.

VANITY

CL.

STEP

CURB

MASTER BED RM.
13'0 x 15'2

TUB

56'-0"

PORCH

BATH

SEAT

GARAGE
21'4 x 21'8

Second Floor

ROOF

ATTIC

OPEN TO GATHERING RM. BELOW

SLOPED CEILING

RAILING

B.

BED RM.
10'4 x 14'0

CL.

LOUNGE
19'4 x 11'10

DN.

BED RM.
18'0 x 13'6

WALK-IN CLOSET

BATH

CL.

TRELLIS

ROOF

ROOF

Design S 2701

1,901 Sq. Ft. – First Floor
891 Sq. Ft. – Second Floor / 50,830 Cu. Ft.

A snack bar in the kitchen! Plus a breakfast nook and formal dining room. Whether it's an elegant dinner party or a quick lunch, this home provides the right spot. There's a wet bar in the family room. Built-in bookcases in the study. And between these two rooms, a gracious fireplace. Three large bedrooms. Including a luxury master suite. Plus a balcony lounge. This home is full of delightful extras.

Design S 2299

1,281 Sq. Ft. – Upper Level
1,320 Sq. Ft. – Lower Level
30,817 Cu. Ft.

A dramatically simple, contemporary bi-level, or split-foyer, home. This rather geometric design is as interesting and distinctive on the inside as on the outside. Double front doors open to a well-lighted entry made possible by the large glass panel above. Down six steps is the main living level. Across the back and functioning with the rear terrace are the spacious formal and informal living areas. A massive two-way fireplace may be enjoyed from each room. The kitchen is most efficient and is but a step from the nook. The laundry and wash room are nearby. The study, or TV room, will surely be a popular haven. Up eight steps from the front entry is the four bedroom, two bath upper level. A balcony looks out upon the sloping ceiling and down into the lower level living areas. The master bedroom has a dressing room and is adjacent to a sizeable storage area. This will be a handy spot to store all the seasonal paraphernalia a large family falls heir to. Bi-level living will be fun here.

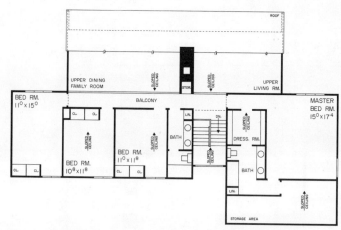

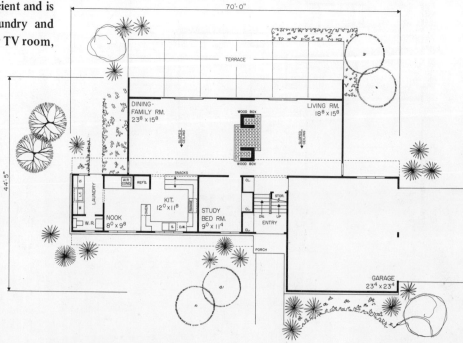

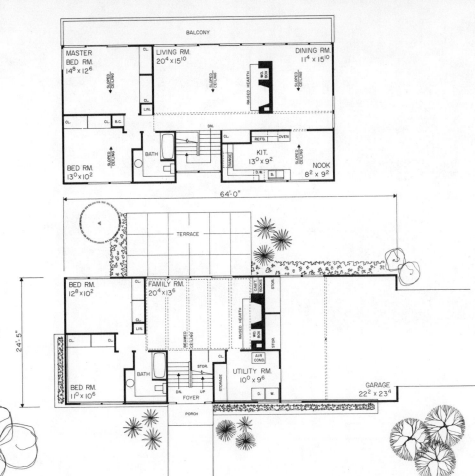

Design S 2319

1,343 Sq. Ft. — Upper Level
980 Sq. Ft. — Lower Level
23,290 Cu. Ft.

This rectangular bi-level home will be most economical to build. The wide overhanging, low-pitched roof enhances the appeal of the exterior. Notice how the upper level, in turn overhangs the lower level. Your investment dollar delivers tremendous livability. There are four bedrooms (two on each level); a family activities area, plus a more formal living room with an adjacent dining room; a fine functioning kitchen opening into the breakfast nook; two raised hearth fireplaces; a sizeable utility room and two-car garage. Be sure to observe the sloping ceilings of the upper level and the beamed ceiling of the family room. Don't miss the sweeping outdoor balcony which provides the main level with an outdoor living facility.

123

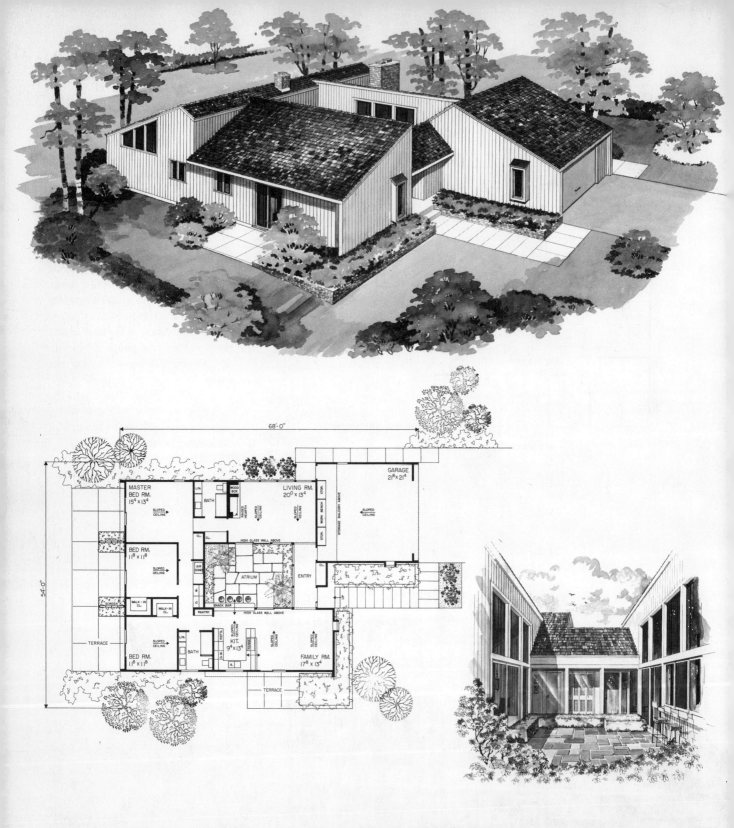

Design S 2182
1,558 Sq. Ft./280 Sq. Ft. Atrium/18,606 Cu. Ft.

What a great new dimension in living is represented by this unique contemporary design! Each of the major zones comprise a separate unit which, along with the garage, clusters around the atrium. High sloped ceilings and plenty of glass areas assure a feeling of spaciousness. The quiet living room will enjoy its privacy, while activities in the informal family room will be great fun functioning with the kitchen. A snack bar opens the kitchen to the atrium. The view at above right shows portions of snack bar and the front entry looking through the glass wall. There are two full baths strategically located to service all areas conveniently. Storage facilities are excellent, indeed. Don't miss the storage potential found in the garage. There is a work bench and storage balcony above.

124

The Informal Lifestyle of Vacation Homes

Design S 2481

1,160 Sq. Ft. — First Floor
828 Sq. Ft. — Second Floor
18,018 Cu. Ft.

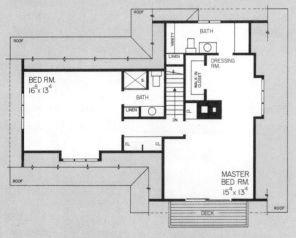

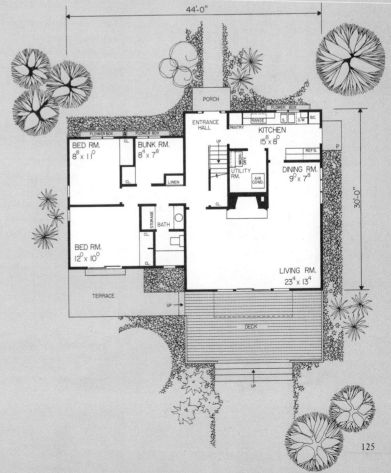

Here is something refreshingly different in the way of vacation home living. Its delightful, barn-like exterior appeal is complimented by its exceptional indoor livability. Just imagine the weekend gang this plan can accommodate! Five bedrooms, three full baths, full-sized kitchen and a spacious living-dining area. Then there is the big deck for outdoor living enjoyment.

New Dimension For Leisure Living

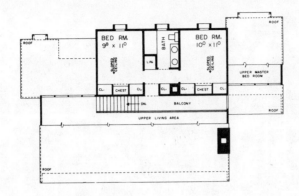

Design S 2472 1,384 Sq. Ft.—First Floor/436 Sq. Ft.—Upper Level/22,127 Cu. Ft.

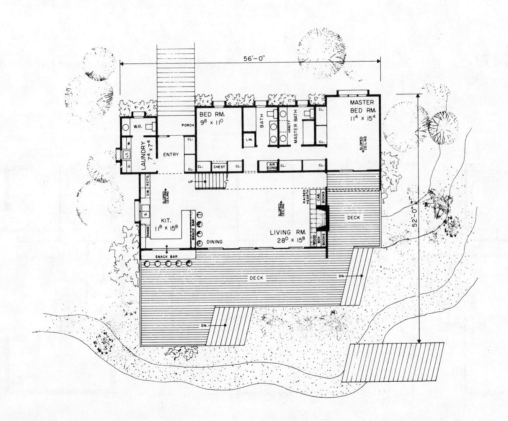

What a refreshing appearance this angular vacation home has! Its contemporary character is accentuated by the various roof planes and the effective window treatment. Inside, the sloping ceilings and the clerestory windows contribute to a dramatic feeling of spaciousness. Whatever your view it will be enjoyed to the fullest from the 28 foot informal living area and kitchen. Sliding glass doors open onto the large deck. A delightful feature is the outdoor snack bar directly accessible from the kitchen. There is a separate laundry with extra wash room nearby. The master bedroom has its own private bath, plenty of closets and direct access to the deck. Two additional full baths serve the three other bedrooms. The upper level balcony looks down on the living area. There are many other features. Try listing them all.

Design S 2471   1,217 Sq. Ft.—Main Level/781 Sq. Ft.—Upper Level/1,204 Sq. Ft.—Lower Level/29,002 Cu. Ft.

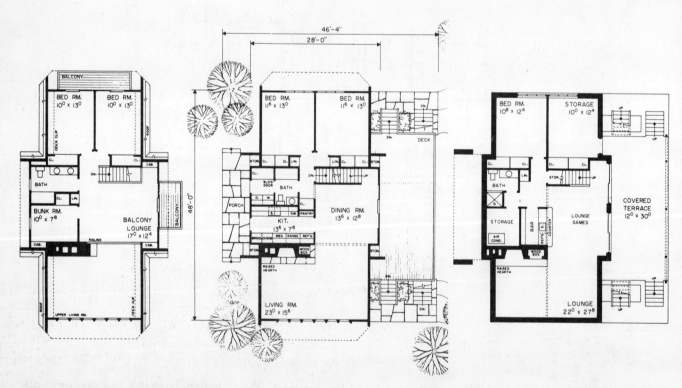

Whatever the scene - spring, summer, fall or (as above) winter - the dramatic appeal of this modified A-frame will be unsurpassed. And little wonder, too. The exterior with its distinctive roof lines, its outstanding window treatment, its big deck, its covered terrace, and its upper level balconies is captivating. The interior, with its long list of features is no less unique. Consider, first of all, the various living areas. Each level has its informal lounging area. Then, there are the excellent sleeping facilities highlighted by five bedrooms, plus a bunk room! Each level has a full bath and plenty of storage. For the storing of skiing equipment and boating gear there is even a separate storage room. Don't miss efficient kitchen and dining room. Eating deck is nearby.

Design S 2469   720 Sq. Ft.—First Floor/483 Sq. Ft.—Upper Level/10,512 Cu. Ft.

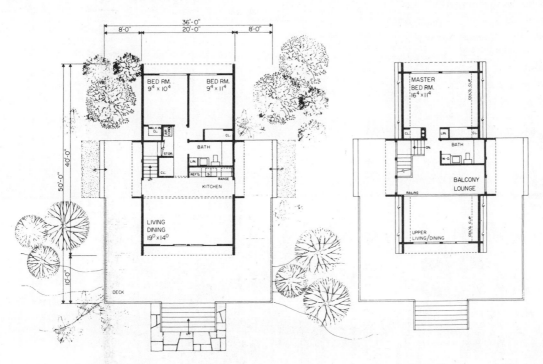

If yours is a hankering for a truly distinctive second home of modest size with excellent livability, and tailored for the moderate building budget, this pleasingly proportioned design may just satisfy your specifications. This 20' x 40' rectangle certainly has its own flair of individuality. Its raised deck and railing add that extra measure of appeal. The projecting roof and sidewalls create a protective recess for the dramatic wall of glass. Such an expanse of glass provides the living-dining area with an abundance of natural light and helps assure a fine awareness of the outdoors. The kitchen is compact and efficient. While there are two bedrooms and full bath downstairs the master bedroom and bath occupy the upper level. The balcony provides extra lounge space. A favorite spot for some.

Design S 2420

768 Sq. Ft. – Upper Level
768 Sq. Ft. – Lower Level
14,896 Cu. Ft.

Two-level living can be fun any-time. When it comes to two-level living at the lake, seashore, or in the woods, the experience will be positively delightful. Whether indoor or outdoor, family living will have a great opportunity for expression. Note two huge living areas, four bedrooms, two baths.

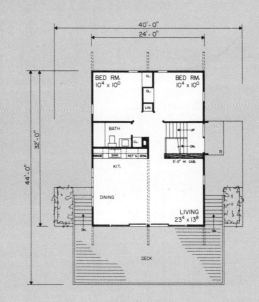

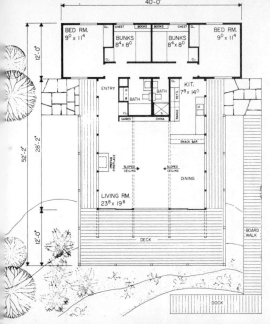

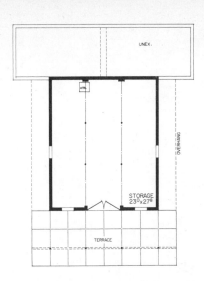

Design S 1410

1165 Sq. Ft. / 17,618 Cu. Ft.

Wherever perched, this cottage will offer interesting and distinctive living patterns. The sleeping zone will enjoy its full measure of privacy. The bunk rooms, and the two larger bedrooms provide plenty of sleeping space. Note the two baths. The cheerful, spacious living area is bounded on three sides by outdoor balcony. The large glass areas, the sloping ceilings, and the exposed beams make this a delightful area. Below the living area is a huge area for boat storage.

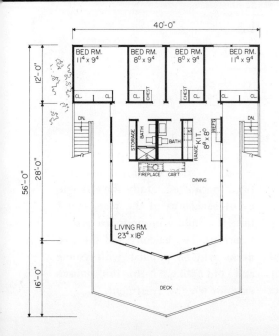

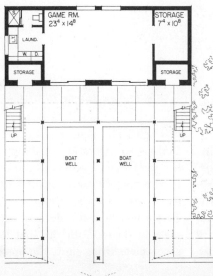

Design S 1429

1,200 Sq. Ft. — Upper Level
646 Sq. Ft. — Lower Level
17,974 Cu. Ft.

Build this week-end home right on the water. With two slips as part of its lower level, this design is a boating enthusiast's dream. Even those left behind after the boat has gone, will love every moment spent relaxing on the upper deck with the water but a few feet below.

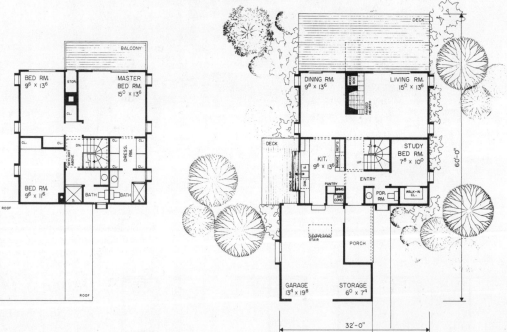

Design S 2477   784 Sq. Ft. - First Floor / 784 Sq. Ft. - Second Floor / 14,683 Cu. Ft.

A most interesting leisure-time home whose exterior is as pleasingly dramatic as its interior is delightfully different. The living unit is a perfect square measuring 28 X 28 feet. The roof is flat and has a skylight unit which provides the spacious stairwell with an abundance of cheerful, natural light. The angular garage is a refreshing configuration. A disappearing stair permits access to the overhead storage area. Clerestory windows assure plenty of natural light. This would be a fine design to complete in stages. With the first floor a complete living unit, the upstairs could be finished-off as time and funds permitted. Study the efficiency of each area of the plan. Don't miss the indoor-outdoor living relationships. The balcony and the two decks will be popular with young and old alike. Note the unique exterior window treatment.

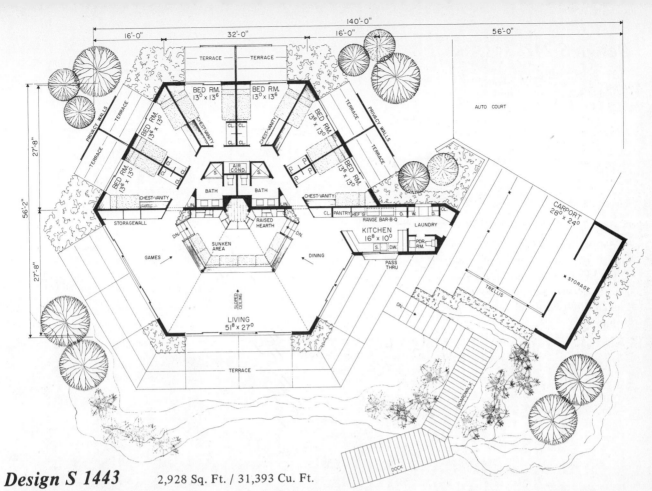

Design S 1443   2,928 Sq. Ft. / 31,393 Cu. Ft.

Is yours a big family? If so, you'll find the living and sleeping accommodations offered by this interesting hexagon exceptional, indeed. The spacious living area features plenty of glass and sliding doors which permit maximum enjoyment of the outdoors from within. A sunken area, with built-in furniture in front of the raised hearth fireplace, will be the favorite gathering spot. The sleeping area consists of six bedrooms. Built-in bunks would permit the sleeping of as many as 24 persons. Observe how each bedroom functions through sliding glass doors with its own outdoor terrace. Note the closet facilities and the built-in chest-vanity in each room. Two centrally located baths highlight twin lavatories and stall showers.

Design S 2478

1,137 Sq. Ft. — First Floor
257 Sq. Ft. — Second Floor
16,218 Cu. Ft.

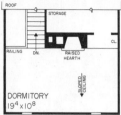

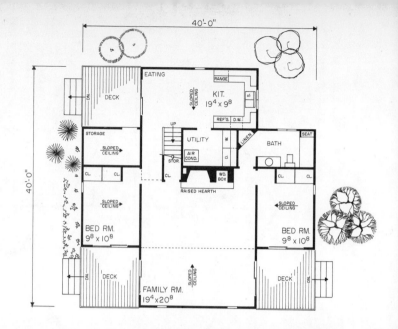

An appealing geometric exterior with a fine floor plan for informal family living. Note the three decks, the big family room, the spacious kitchen, the two fireplaces, and the dormitory.

Design S 2480

826 Sq. Ft. — First Floor
533 Sq. Ft. — Second Floor
14,650 Cu. Ft.

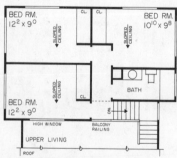

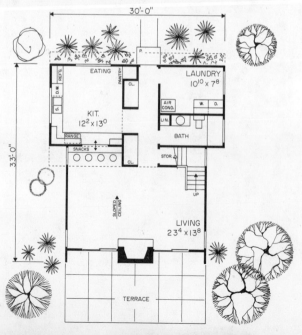

This distinctive contemporary two-story leisure-time home provides excellent living patterns. Observe efficient kitchen, separate laundry, sloped ceilinged living room, two baths, and three bedrooms.

134

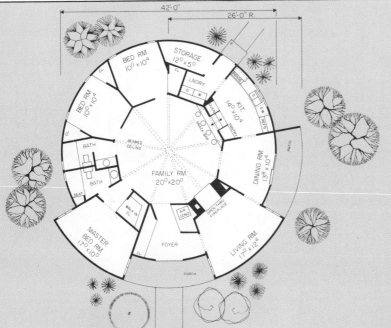

Design S 2479

1,547 Sq. Ft. / 14,878 Cu. Ft.

Here is a unique round house with an equally unique floor plan. The centrally located family room is the focal point around which the various family functions and activities revolve. There is much to study and admire in this plan. For instance, the use of space is most efficient. Notice the strategic location of the kitchen. Don't miss the storage room and laundry. Observe the snack bar, the two-way fireplace, the separate dining room and the two full baths. Fixed glass windows at the beamed ceiling provides natural light from above for the family room.

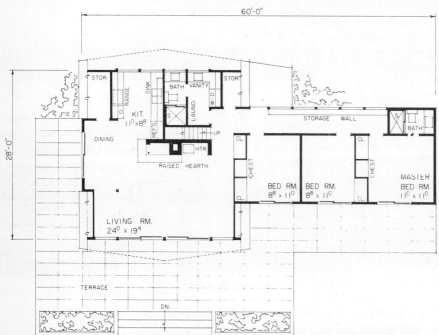

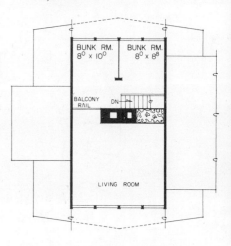

Design S 1408

1.296 Sq. Ft. — First Floor
181 Sq. Ft. — Second Floor
12,248 Cu. Ft.

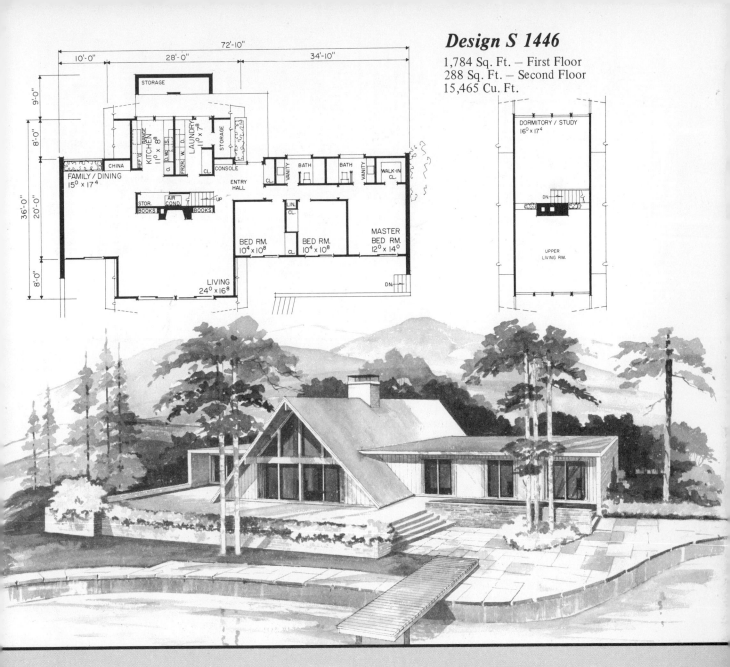

Design S 1446

1,784 Sq. Ft. — First Floor
288 Sq. Ft. — Second Floor
15,465 Cu. Ft.

First Floor dimensions and labels:

72'-10"
10'-0" 28'-0" 34'-10"
9'-0" 8'-0" 36'-0" 20'-0" 8'-0"

STORAGE
KITCHEN 11⁰ x 8⁸
LAUNDRY 11⁷ x 7⁸
STORAGE
REF'G. RANGE FRZR. W. D.
CHINA
CL.
CONSOLE
VANITY BATH BATH VANITY WALK-IN CL.
CL. CL.
FAMILY / DINING 15⁰ x 17⁴
STOR. AIR COND. UP
BOOKS BOOKS
ENTRY HALL
LIN. CL.
BED RM. 10⁴ x 10⁸
BED RM. 10⁴ x 10⁸
CL.
MASTER BED RM. 12⁰ x 14⁰
LIVING 24⁰ x 16⁸
DN.

Second Floor:

DORMITORY / STUDY 16⁰ x 17⁴
DN.
UPPER LIVING RM.

Design S 1448

776 Sq. Ft. — First Floor
300 Sq. Ft. — Second Floor
8,596 Cu. Ft.

First Floor dimensions and labels:

24'-0"
32'-0"
16'-0"

BED RM. 11⁶ x 11⁰
STOR.
BATH
LIN.
REF'G. RANGE
S.
KITCHEN 11⁶ x 7⁸
CL. CL. STORAGE
UP
DINING
LIVING 23⁶ x 15⁸
DN. DN.
DECK

Second Floor:

BALCONY ROOF
DORMITORY 15⁰ x 16⁰
STOR. CL.
DN.
BALCONY
UPPER LIVING
ROOF

Here are three dramatic A-frames designed to fit varying budgets and family living requirements. Compare the size of Design S 1448 at left with that of S 1446 above. While the difference in livability features is great, so is the difference in construction costs. However, the significance each design represents to the family's basic life style is similar. The proud owners of either home will enjoy all the benefits and experiences that come from leisure-time, second home living. Study the interior of S 1408. It, too, has much to offer the fun oriented family.

137

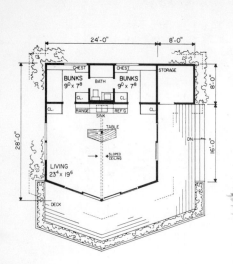

Design S 1403 698 Sq. Ft./7,441 Cu. Ft.

Here are five outstanding second homes which, in spite of their variation in size, have many things in common. Perhaps the most significant common denominator is the location of the living area and its unrestricted view of the outdoors. Each of the designs feature a glass gable end and sloping ceiling which assures the living zone of a bright and cheerful atmosphere. A study of the sizes and the livability of these designs is interesting. They range in size from a 576 square foot, one bedroom cottage, to a 1,456 square foot lodge with four bedrooms plus two bunk rooms. Regardless of the overall size of the interior, the open planning of the living areas results in plenty of space for your family and visitors to just sit around and talk.

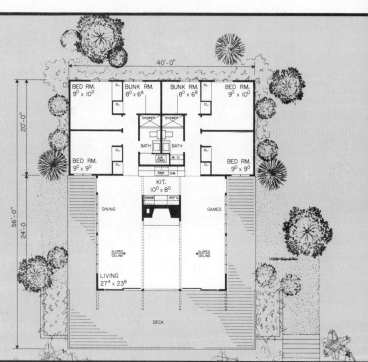

Design S 2423 864 Sq. Ft./9,504 Cu. Ft.

Design S 1458 576 Sq. Ft./5,904 Cu. Ft.

Design S 2424

1,456 Sq. Ft./16,760 Cu. Ft.

Design S 1495 800 Sq. Ft./9,108 Cu. Ft.

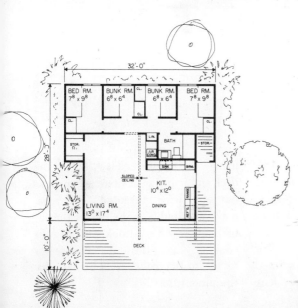

Design S 2470
1,226 Sq. Ft.—Upper Level/805 Sq. Ft.—Lower Level/20,210 Cu. Ft.

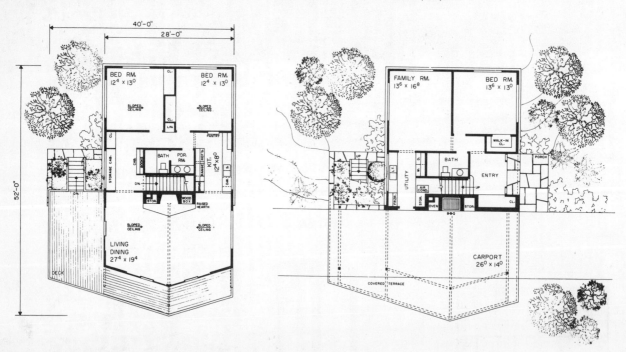

You will enter this vacation home on the lower level. Here, the main entry routes traffic to the family room and extra bedroom - make it a bunk room if you wish. A full bath is centrally located. Then, up a full flight of stairs to the main living level. With all those windows and the sloped ceilings there is a feeling of great spaciousness. The focal point of the 27 foot living area will be the raised hearth fireplaces. Traffic will flow easily to and from the outdoor deck as a result of the three sets of slidings glass doors. The efficient kitchen and good storage facilities will help assure convenient living. On the lower level, below the deck and living area, there is excellent outdoor living potential. This area, may also double as shelter for the car or boat. Don't overlook the outdoor cooking facilities or the access to the utility room with its laundry equipment.

Design S 1457

640 Sq. Ft.—Upper Level/640 Sq. Ft.—Lower Level/11,712 Cu. Ft.

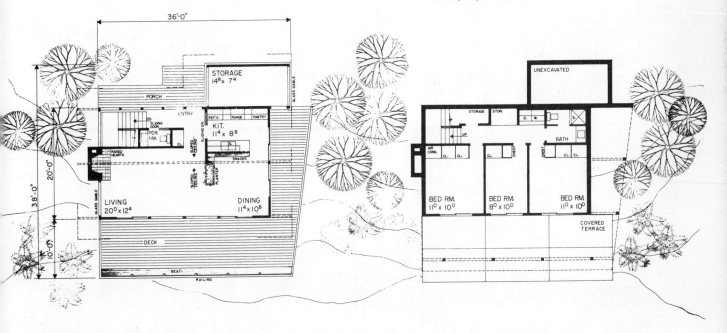

This hillside vacation home seems to just grow right out of its sloping site. It, therefore, is putting its site to the best possible use. As a result of being able to expose the lower level the total livable floor area of the house is doubled. This is truly the most practical and economical manner by which to increase livability so dramatically. The upper level is the living level. This is just where you want to be during the day when there is a delightful view to be enjoyed from a high vantage point. For outdoor living there is the big deck which wraps around one side of the house. Where swimming is involved dressing rooms are nearby.

141

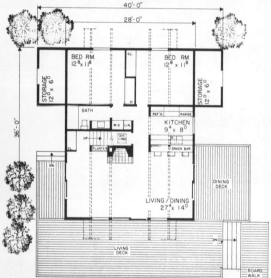

Design S 1444

1,008 Sq. Ft.—First Floor
624 Sq. Ft.—Second Floor
15,542 Cu. Ft.

Everybody will have fun spending their vacations at this cottage. And why shouldn't they? The pleasant experiences of vacation living will be more than just sitting on the outdoor balconies of the second floor. They will include eating leisurely on the dining deck and lounging peacefully on the living deck. Further, they will encompass the relaxing hours spent before the cheerful fireplace on cool evenings. For privacy there are four bedrooms.

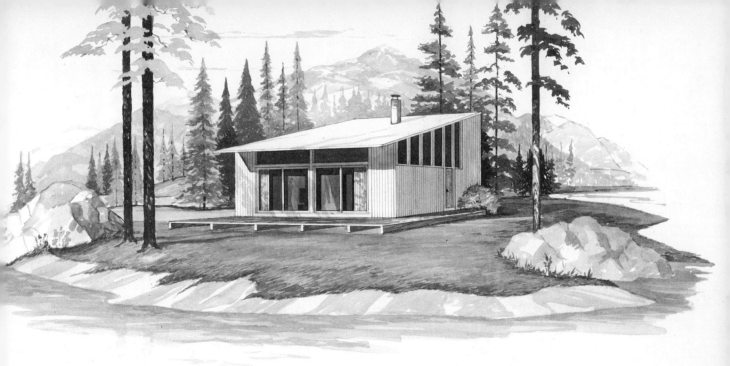

Design S 1496

768 Sq. Ft.—First Floor
288 Sq. Ft.—Second Floor
15,840 Cu. Ft.

If your vacation home desires include the wish for something distinctive in the way of exterior design, you'll find this unique home a tempting choice. The overhanging shed roof, the interesting glass areas, and the vertical siding help create an attractive facade. Inside, the living area is big and spacious. Each floor features a good sized bedroom with a full bath nearby. The ceiling is sloped and has exposed beams.

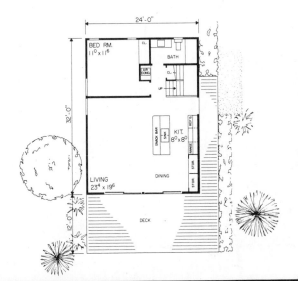

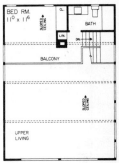

Design S 1427

1,008 Sq. Ft.—First Floor/688 Sq. Ft.
Second Floor/18,648 Cu. Ft.

Imagine yourself living in this outstanding vacation home. Whether located deep in the woods or along the shore line, you will forever be aware of your glorious surroundings. As you relax in your living room you will enjoy the massive, raised hearth fireplace, the high-pitched beamed ceiling, the broad expanses of glass and the dramatic balcony looking down from above. List the features.

143

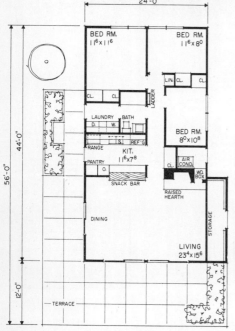

Design S 1459

1,056 Sq. Ft.–First Floor / 400 Sq. Ft.
Second Floor / 17,504 Cu. Ft.

There is a heap of vacation living awaiting the gang that descends upon this smart looking chalet adaptation. If you have a narrow site, this design will be of extra interest to you. Should one of your requirements be abundant sleeping facilities, you'd hardly do better in such an economically built design. There are three bedrooms downstairs. A ladder leads to the second floor loft. The children will love the idea of sleeping here. In addition, there is a play area which looks down upon the first floor living room.

Design S 2427

784 Sq. Ft.–First Floor/504 Sq. Ft.
Second Floor/13,485 Cu. Ft.

If ever a design had "vacation home" written all over it, this one has! Perhaps the most carefree characteristic of all is the second floor balcony which looks down upon the wood deck. This balcony provides the outdoor living facility for the big master bedroom. Also occupying the second floor is the kids' dormitory. The use of bunks would be a fine utilization of this space. Panels through the knee walls give access to abundant storage area. Downstairs there is yet another bedroom, a full bath and a 27 foot living room.

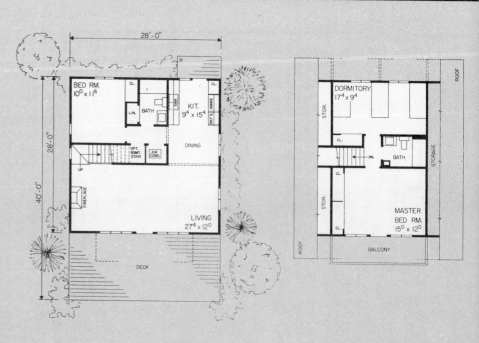

Design S 1424

672 Sq. Ft.—First Floor / 256 Sq. Ft.
Second Floor / 8,736 Cu. Ft.

This chalet-type vacation home with its steep, overhanging roof, will catch the eye of even the most casual on-looker. It is designed to be completely livable whether the season be for swimming or skiing. The dormitory of upper level will sleep many vacationers, while the two bedrooms of the first floor provide the more convenient and conventional sleeping facilities. The upper level overlooks the living and dining area with its beamed ceiling. The lower level functions well and provides everything that one would want for vacation living.

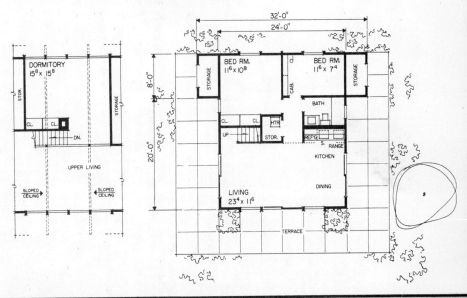

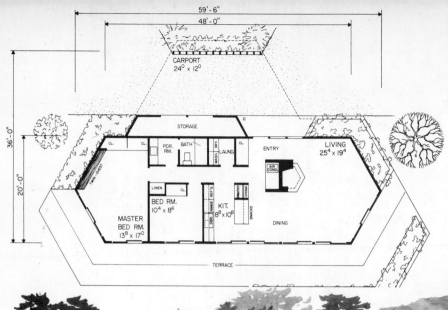

Your setting for this refreshing six-sided home may differ tremendously from the picture below. But, whatever the character of the surroundings, the flair of distinction and the degree of livability will not change. This is truly a home away from home. As you welcome the new living patterns, you will also embrace the delightful change of pace. There are eight sets of sliding glass doors which facilitate passage in-and-out-of-doors.

Design S 2421

1,075 Sq. Ft./10,548 Cu. Ft.

Design S 1439

1,284 Sq. Ft./11,338 Cu. Ft.

This handsome contemporary house is a far cry from the rough cabins we sometimes envision as vacation houses. It's truly designed for big family living, with four bedrooms, two baths, and a standard-sized kitchen. It also has the essential ingredients for cutting down maintenance, such as weathered board-and-batten siding and a windproof flat roof. There are many floor-to-ceiling windows to bring in the summer sunlight, but overhangs keeps out the sun's heat.

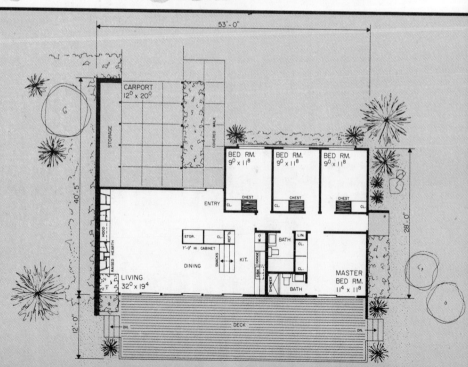

Design S 1497

1,292 Sq. Ft./14,274 Cu. Ft.

Another design whose general shape is most interesting and whose livability is truly refreshing. After a stay in this fine second home it will, indeed, be difficult to resume your daily activities in your first home. When you return from vacation you will surely miss the spaciousness of your living room, the efficiency of your work center, the pleasing layout of your master bedroom, and all those glass sliding doors which mean you are usually but a step from out-of-doors.

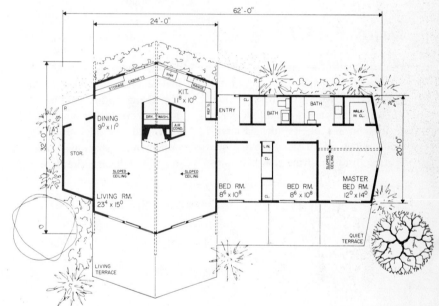

Design S 1451 1,224 Sq. Ft.–First Floor/464 Sq. Ft.–Second Floor/15,912 Cu. Ft.

This dramatic A-frame will surely command its share of attention wherever located. Its soaring roof and large glass areas put this design in a class all of its own. Raised wood decks on all sides provide delightful outdoor living areas. In addition, there is a balcony outside the second floor master bedroom. The living room will be the focal point of the interior. With all that glass and the high roof it will be wonderfully spacious. The attractive raised hearth fireplace will be a favorite feature. Another favored highlight will be the lounge area of the second floor from which it is possible to look down into the living room. The work center has all the conveniences of home. Note the barbeque unit, pantry and china.

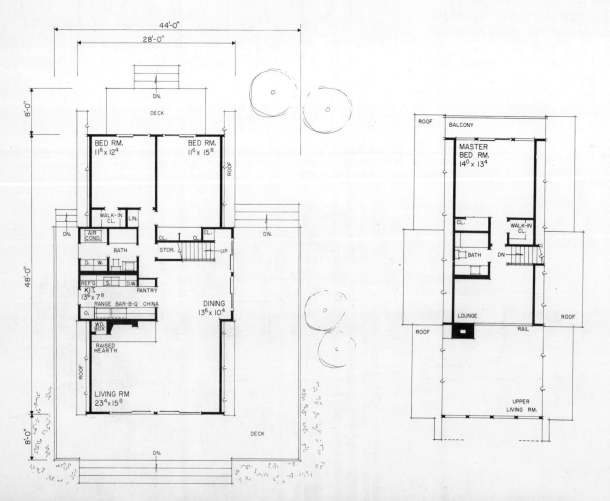

The Economy of Medium & Low-Cost Homes

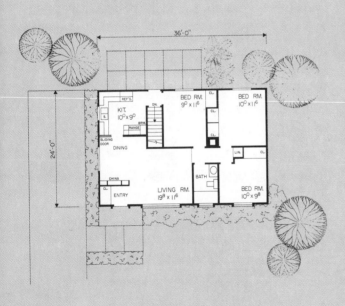

Design S 2167

864 Sq. Ft. / 16,554 Cu. Ft.

This 36' x 24' contemporary rectangle will be economical to build whether you construct the basement design at left, S 2167, or the non-basement version below, S 2168.

Design S 2168

864 Sq. Ft. / 9,244 Cu. Ft.

This non-basement design features a storage room and a laundry area with cupboards above the washer and dryer. Notice the kitchen eating space.

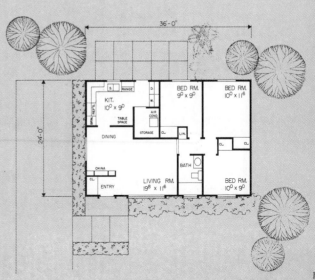

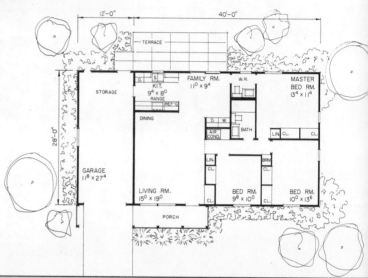

Design S 1187

1,120 Sq. Ft. / 12,600 Cu. Ft.

Just think, from a perfect rectangle, such an attractive house with such a fine living potential. Note the oversized garage for storage of bulk items.

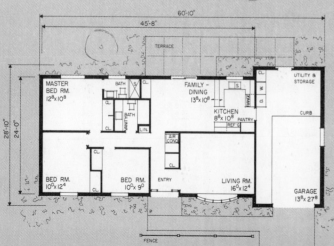

Design S 1364

1,142 Sq. Ft. / 13,510 Cu. Ft.

Two full baths, a separate family-dining area, a pass-thru to the efficient U-shaped kitchen and good storage facilities are among highlights of this design.

OPTIONAL BASEMENT PLAN

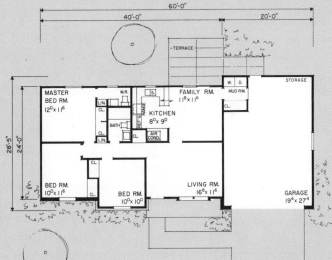

Design S 1311

1,040 Sq. Ft. / 11,370 Cu. Ft.

The blueprints you order for this design include details for both basement and non-basement construction. Observe the interesting variations in the two plans.

Design S 1309

1,100 Sq. Ft. / 15,600 Cu. Ft.

An efficient kitchen is flanked by an informal family room and a formal dining room. Exterior is essentially frame with boards and battens and horizontal siding.

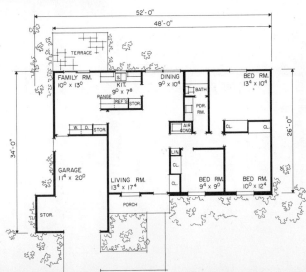

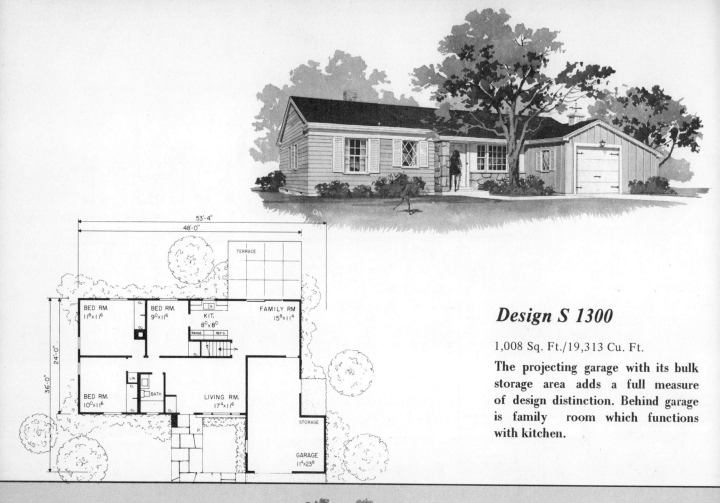

Design S 1300

1,008 Sq. Ft./19,313 Cu. Ft.

The projecting garage with its bulk storage area adds a full measure of design distinction. Behind garage is family room which functions with kitchen.

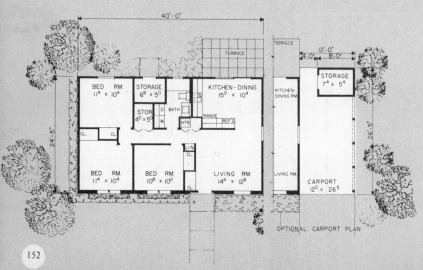

Design S 3221

976 Sq. Ft./9,523 Cu. Ft.

This hip-roof home has a wide overhang. Plan features excellent storage facilities. The kitchen-dining area is spacious and overlooks rear yard.

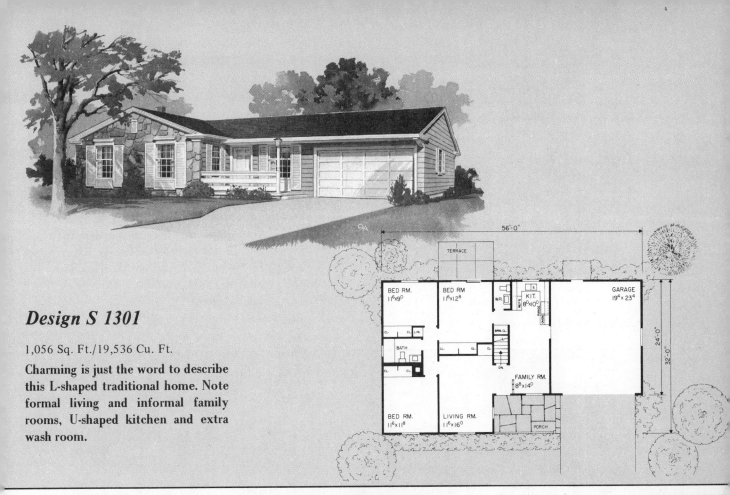

Design S 1301

1,056 Sq. Ft./19,536 Cu. Ft.

Charming is just the word to describe this L-shaped traditional home. Note formal living and informal family rooms, U-shaped kitchen and extra wash room.

Design S 3223

1,022 Sq. Ft./12,264 Cu. Ft.

The master bedroom of this efficient plan has direct access to the wash room. The kitchen is but a few steps from the rear yard.

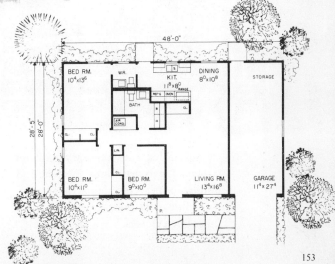

153

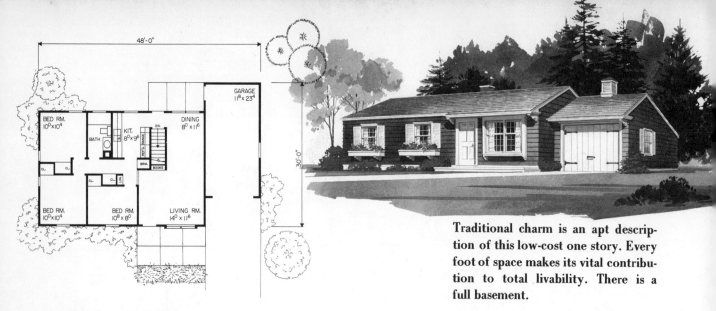

Design S 2163   864 Sq. Ft./16,554 Cu. Ft.

Traditional charm is an apt description of this low-cost one story. Every foot of space makes its vital contribution to total livability. There is a full basement.

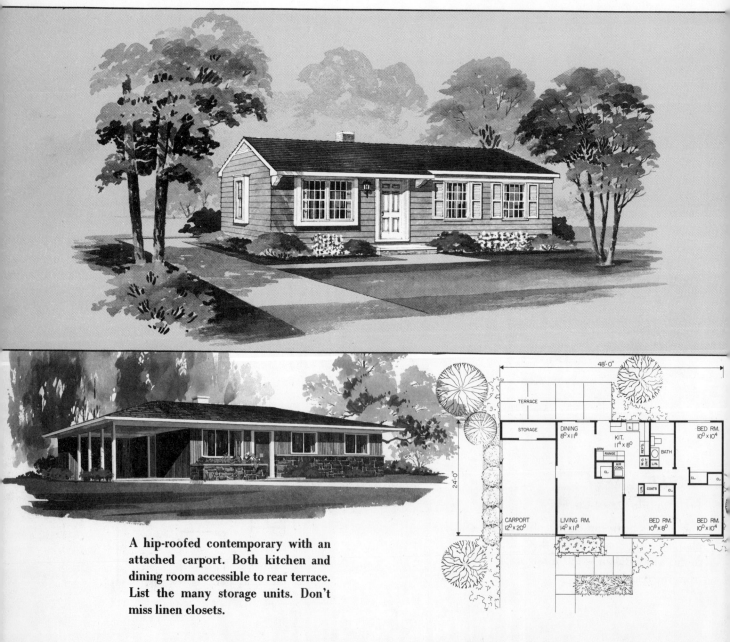

A hip-roofed contemporary with an attached carport. Both kitchen and dining room accessible to rear terrace. List the many storage units. Don't miss linen closets.

Design S 2166   864 Sq. Ft./8,448 Cu. Ft.

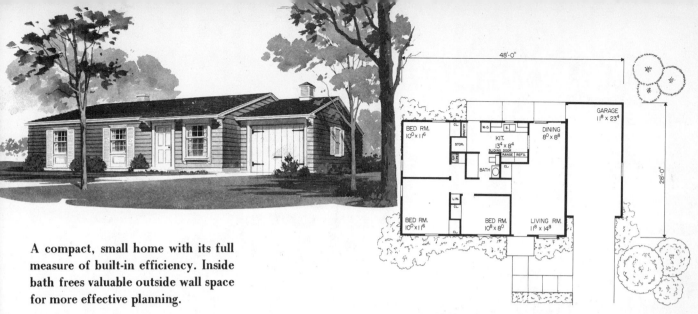

A compact, small home with its full measure of built-in efficiency. Inside bath frees valuable outside wall space for more effective planning.

Design S 2164 864 Sq. Ft./9,245 Cu. Ft.

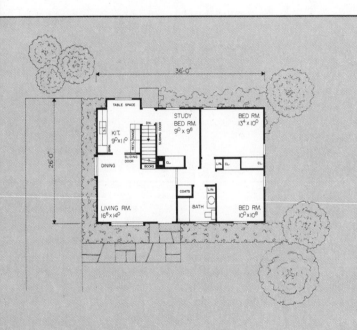

Design S 2165

878 Sq. Ft./16,945 Cu. Ft.

Whether called upon to function as a two or three bedroom home, this attractive design will serve its occupents well. There are two eating areas.

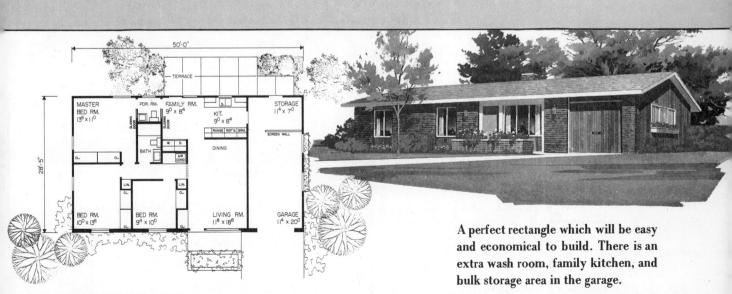

A perfect rectangle which will be easy and economical to build. There is an extra wash room, family kitchen, and bulk storage area in the garage.

Design S 2159 1,077 Sq. Ft./11,222 Cu. Ft.

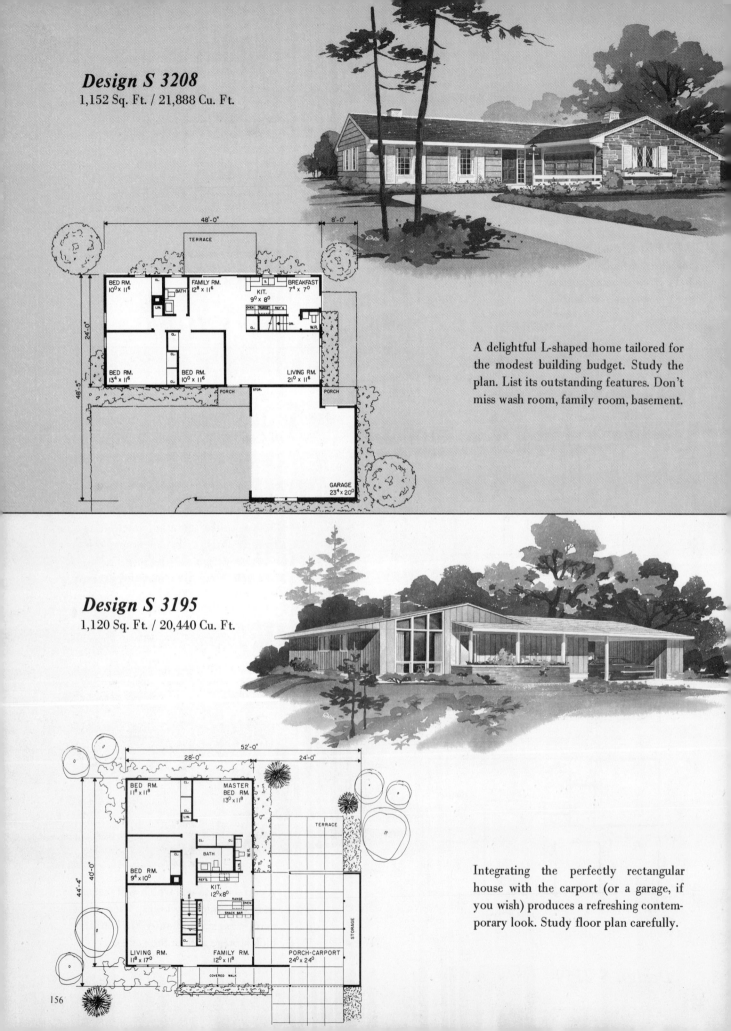

Design S 3208
1,152 Sq. Ft. / 21,888 Cu. Ft.

TERRACE

48'-0"   8'-0"

BED RM. 10⁰ x 11⁶
FAMILY RM. 12⁸ x 11⁶
BATH
KIT. 9⁰ x 8⁰
BREAKFAST 7⁴ x 7⁰
OVEN RANGE REF'G.
LIN.
CL.
DN.
W.R.

24'-0"

BED RM. 13⁴ x 11⁶
CL.
CL.
BED RM. 10⁰ x 11⁶
LIVING RM. 21⁰ x 11⁶

48'-5"

PORCH   STOR.   PORCH

GARAGE 23⁴ x 20⁰

A delightful L-shaped home tailored for the modest building budget. Study the plan. List its outstanding features. Don't miss wash room, family room, basement.

Design S 3195
1,120 Sq. Ft. / 20,440 Cu. Ft.

52'-0"
28'-0"   24'-0"

BED RM. 11⁸ x 11⁸
MASTER BED RM. 13⁰ x 11⁸
CL.
CL.
LIN.

TERRACE

40'-0"

BED RM. 9⁴ x 10⁰
CL.
CL.
BATH
W.R.
REF'G.
KIT. 12⁰ x 8⁰

44'-4"

RANGE
OVEN
SNACK BAR
STOR.
STOR.

STORAGE

LIVING RM. 11⁸ x 17⁰
FAMILY RM. 12⁰ x 11⁸
PORCH-CARPORT 24⁰ x 24⁰

COVERED WALK

Integrating the perfectly rectangular house with the carport (or a garage, if you wish) produces a refreshing contemporary look. Study floor plan carefully.

Design S 1113
1,008 Sq. Ft. / 19,737 Cu. Ft.

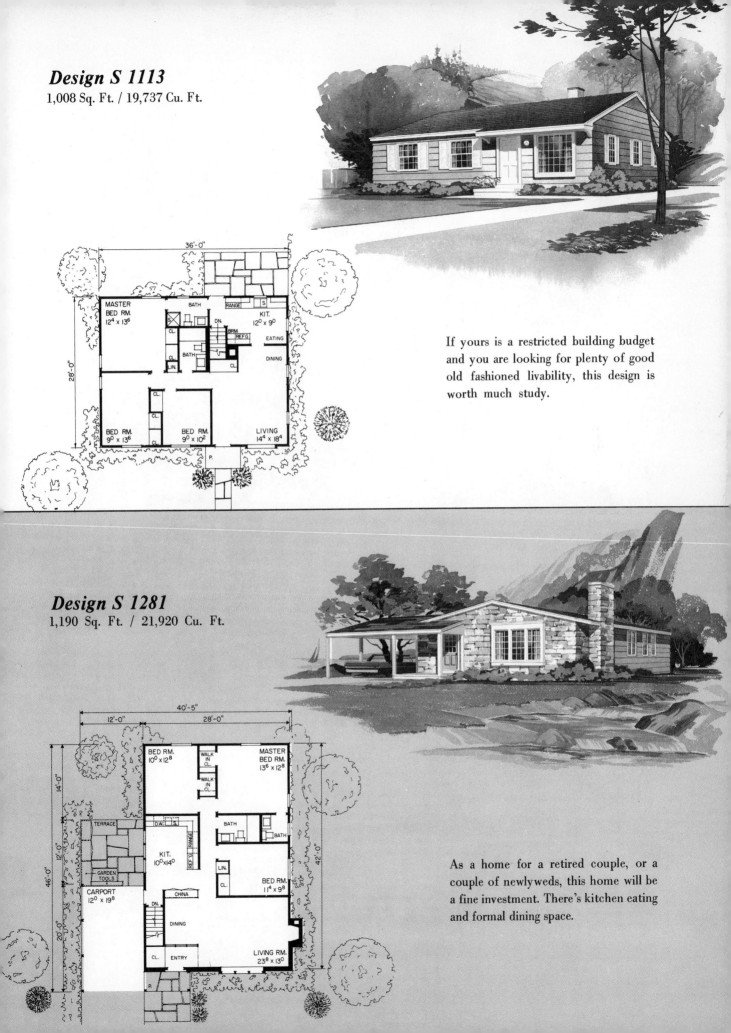

If yours is a restricted building budget and you are looking for plenty of good old fashioned livability, this design is worth much study.

Floor plan — Design S 1113
- 36'-0"
- 28'-0"
- MASTER BED RM. 12⁴ x 13⁶
- BATH
- RANGE S
- KIT. 12⁰ x 9⁰
- DN.
- BRM
- REFG
- EATING
- DINING
- CL.
- BATH
- LIN.
- CL.
- BED RM. 9⁰ x 13⁶
- CL.
- CL.
- CL.
- BED RM. 9⁰ x 10²
- LIVING 14⁴ x 18⁴
- P.

Design S 1281
1,190 Sq. Ft. / 21,920 Cu. Ft.

As a home for a retired couple, or a couple of newlyweds, this home will be a fine investment. There's kitchen eating and formal dining space.

Floor plan — Design S 1281
- 40'-5"
- 12'-0"
- 28'-0"
- 14'-0"
- 12'-0"
- 46'-0"
- 20'-0"
- 42'-0"
- BED RM. 10⁰ x 12⁸
- WALK IN CL.
- MASTER BED RM. 13⁶ x 12⁸
- WALK IN CL.
- TERRACE
- D.W. S
- REF'G RANGE
- BATH
- BATH
- KIT. 10⁰ x 14⁰
- GARDEN TOOLS
- CARPORT 12⁰ x 19⁸
- LIN.
- CL.
- CHINA
- BED RM. 11⁴ x 9⁸
- DN.
- DINING
- CL.
- ENTRY
- LIVING RM. 23⁸ x 13⁰
- P.

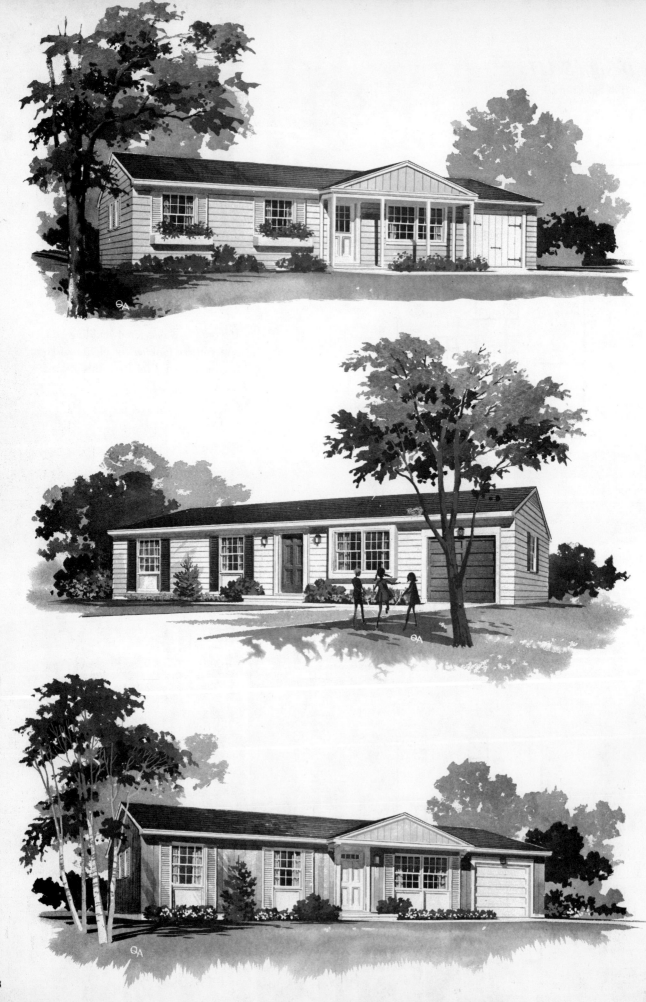

Design S 2153   960 Sq. Ft./18,432 Cu. Ft.

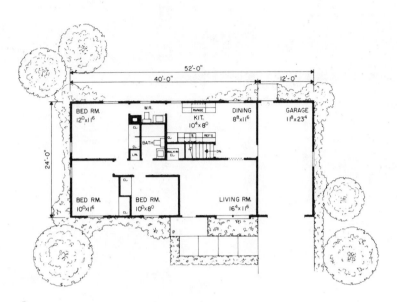

If you can't make up your mind as to which of the delightful traditional exteriors you like best on the opposing page, you need not decide now. The blueprints you receive show details for the construction of all three front exteriors. However, before you order, decide whether you wish your next home to have a basement or not. If you prefer the basement plan order Design S 2153 above. Should your preference be for a non-basement plan you should order blueprints for Design S 2154 below. Whatever your choice, you'll forever love the charm of exterior and the comfort and convenience of the interior.

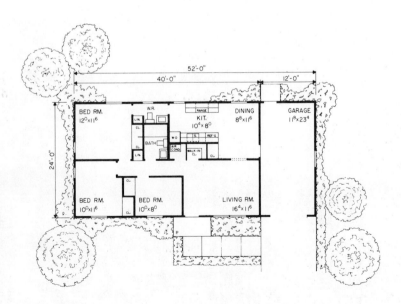

Design S 2154   960 Sq. Ft./18,432 Cu. Ft.

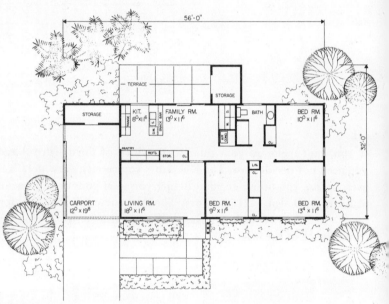

Design S 2158

1,058 Sq. Ft. / 10,749 Cu. Ft.

A fine contemporary with a low-pitched, wide overhanging roof. Note the planters, attached carport (make it a garage, if you wish), and storage areas.

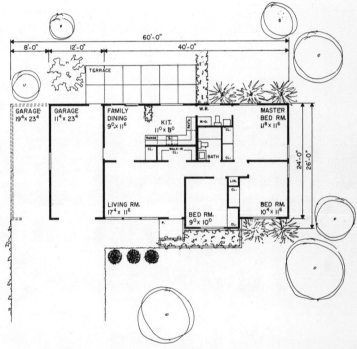

OPTIONAL BASEMENT PLAN

Design S 3196

984 Sq. Ft. / 9,840 Cu. Ft.

There is a heap of living to be enjoyed in this modest home. Observe extra wash room. Plans for this particular design include optional basement.

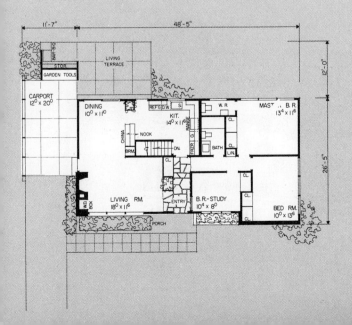

Design S 3164

1,164 Sq. Ft. / 20,370 Cu. Ft.

The master bedroom has private wash room. There are plenty of closets, two built-in planters and a china storage unit. Observe fireplace and wood box.

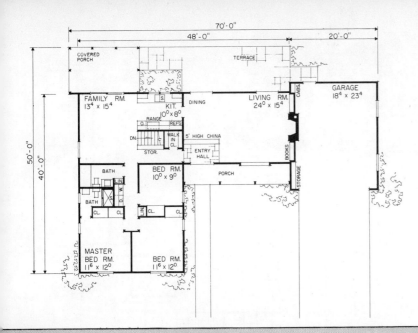

Design S 1074

1,356 Sq. Ft. / 25,431 Cu. Ft.

You'll be thrilled with the selection of this L-shaped traditional as your next home. And little wonder. It has exterior beauty and great interior livability.

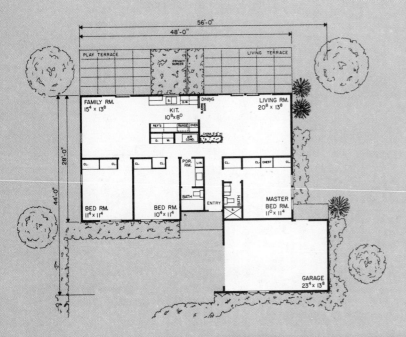

Design S 1188

1,326 Sq. Ft. / 16,469 Cu. Ft.

Here is a unique plan which separates the master bedroom from the children's bedrooms. Kitchen is flanked by informal family room and formal living room.

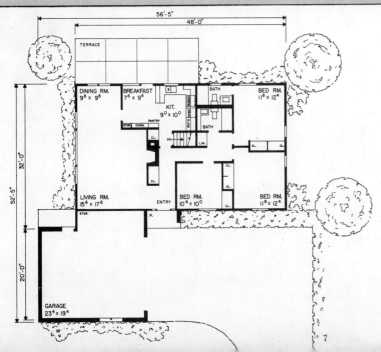

Design S 3211

1,349 Sq. Ft. / 26,423 Cu. Ft.

Here is another captivating version of the three bedroom, L-shaped home. Observe the back-to-back plumbing, the breakfast and dining rooms.

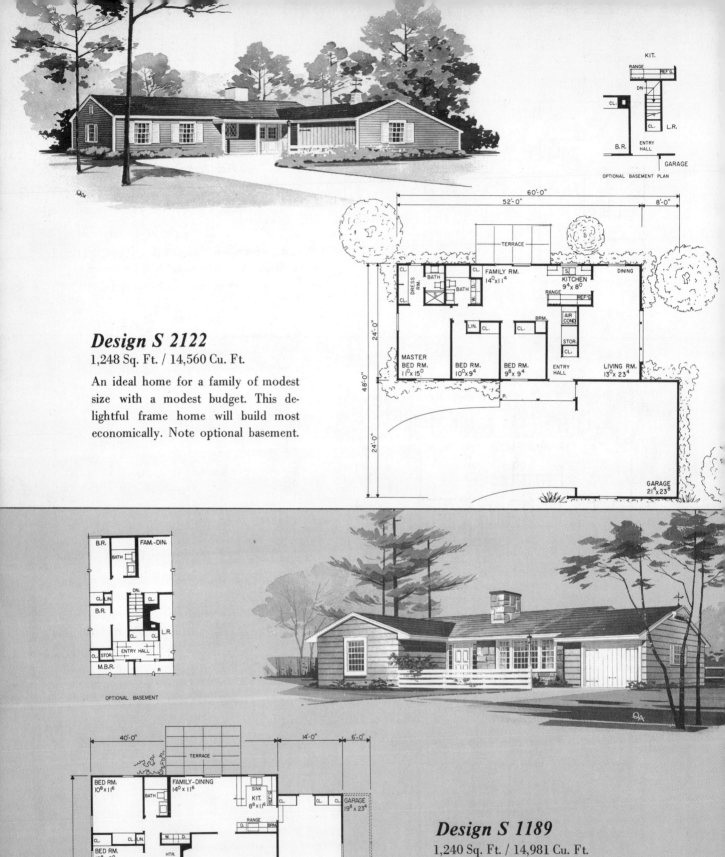

Design S 2122

1,248 Sq. Ft. / 14,560 Cu. Ft.

An ideal home for a family of modest size with a modest budget. This delightful frame home will build most economically. Note optional basement.

Design S 1189

1,240 Sq. Ft. / 14,981 Cu. Ft.

A master bedroom with private bath, an efficient kitchen with pass-thru to family-dining room, and a spacious living room are among the highlights.

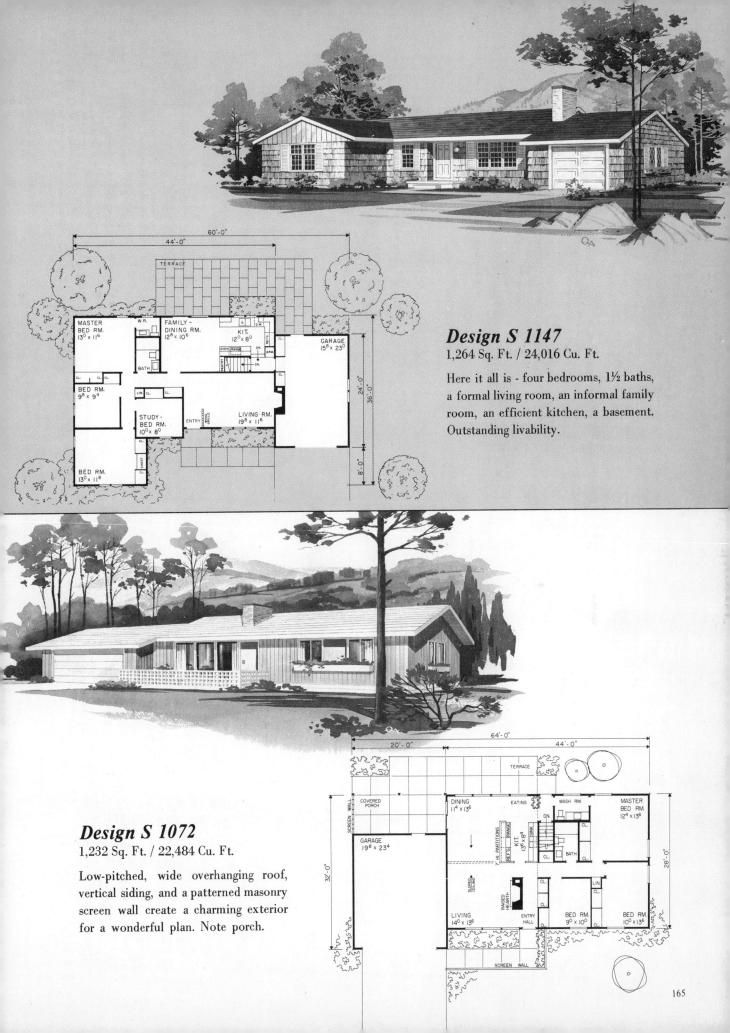

Design S 1147

1,264 Sq. Ft. / 24,016 Cu. Ft.

Here it all is - four bedrooms, 1½ baths, a formal living room, an informal family room, an efficient kitchen, a basement. Outstanding livability.

Design S 1072

1,232 Sq. Ft. / 22,484 Cu. Ft.

Low-pitched, wide overhanging roof, vertical siding, and a patterned masonry screen wall create a charming exterior for a wonderful plan. Note porch.

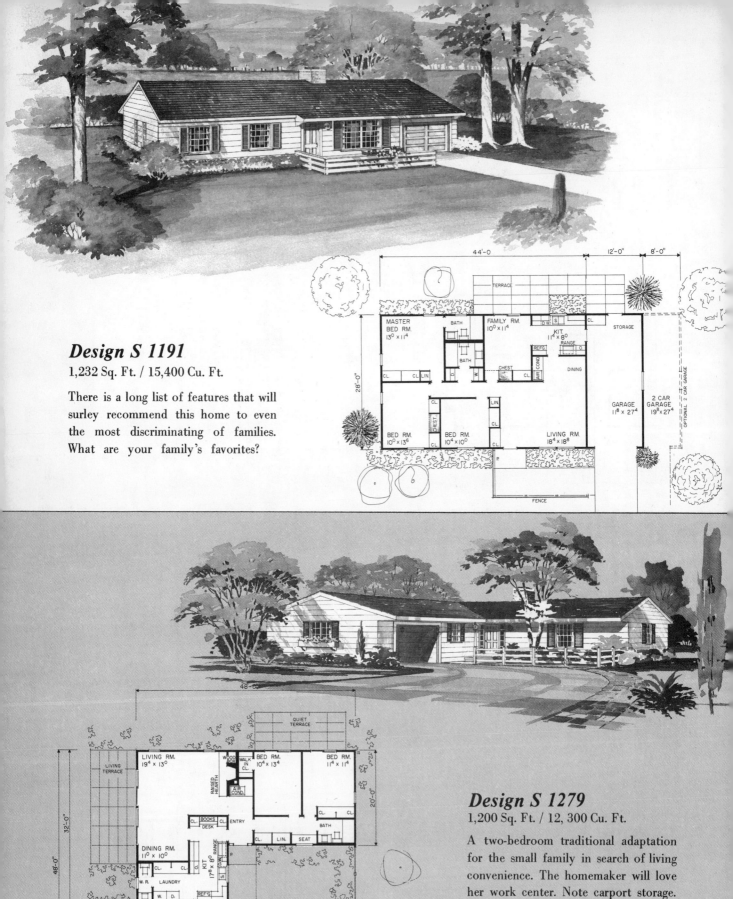

Design S 1191
1,232 Sq. Ft. / 15,400 Cu. Ft.

There is a long list of features that will surley recommend this home to even the most discriminating of families. What are your family's favorites?

Design S 1279
1,200 Sq. Ft. / 12, 300 Cu. Ft.

A two-bedroom traditional adaptation for the small family in search of living convenience. The homemaker will love her work center. Note carport storage.

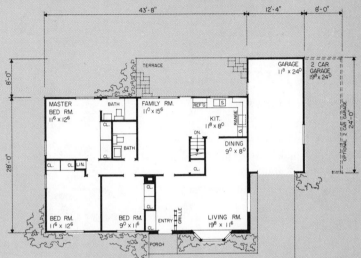

Design S 1075

1,232 Sq. Ft. / 24,123 Cu. Ft.

This picturesque traditional one-story has much to offer the young family. Its rectangular shape means economical construction. Observe two baths.

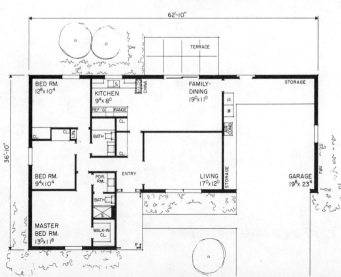

Design S 1366

1,280 Sq. Ft. / 14,848 Cu. Ft.

The center entrance of this three bedroom, two bath L-shaped house routes traffic directly to each of the major areas. Notice privacy of the living room.

167

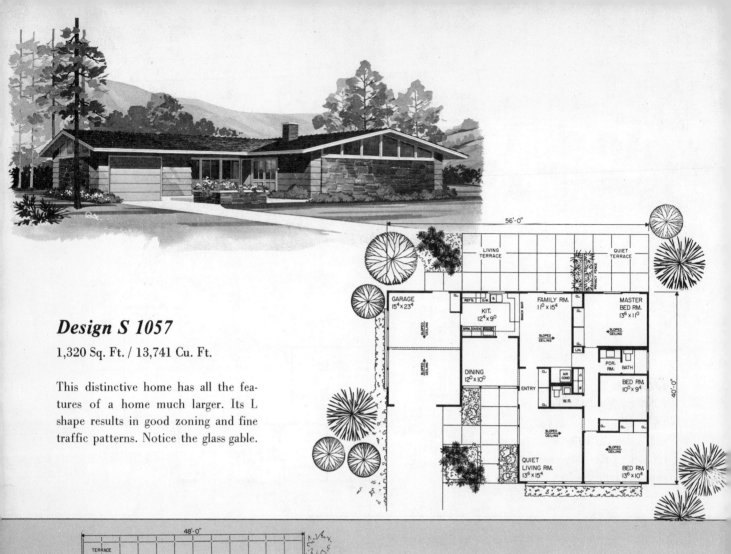

Design S 1057

1,320 Sq. Ft. / 13,741 Cu. Ft.

This distinctive home has all the features of a home much larger. Its L shape results in good zoning and fine traffic patterns. Notice the glass gable.

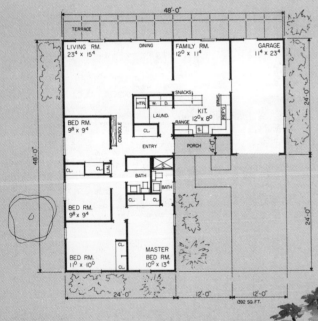

Design S 1327

1,392 Sq. Ft. / 18,480 Cu. Ft.

While adding square footage to a house adds cost, it also adds livibility. Here there are four bedrooms, two baths, large formal and informal living areas.

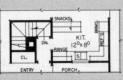

OPTIONAL BASEMENT PLAN

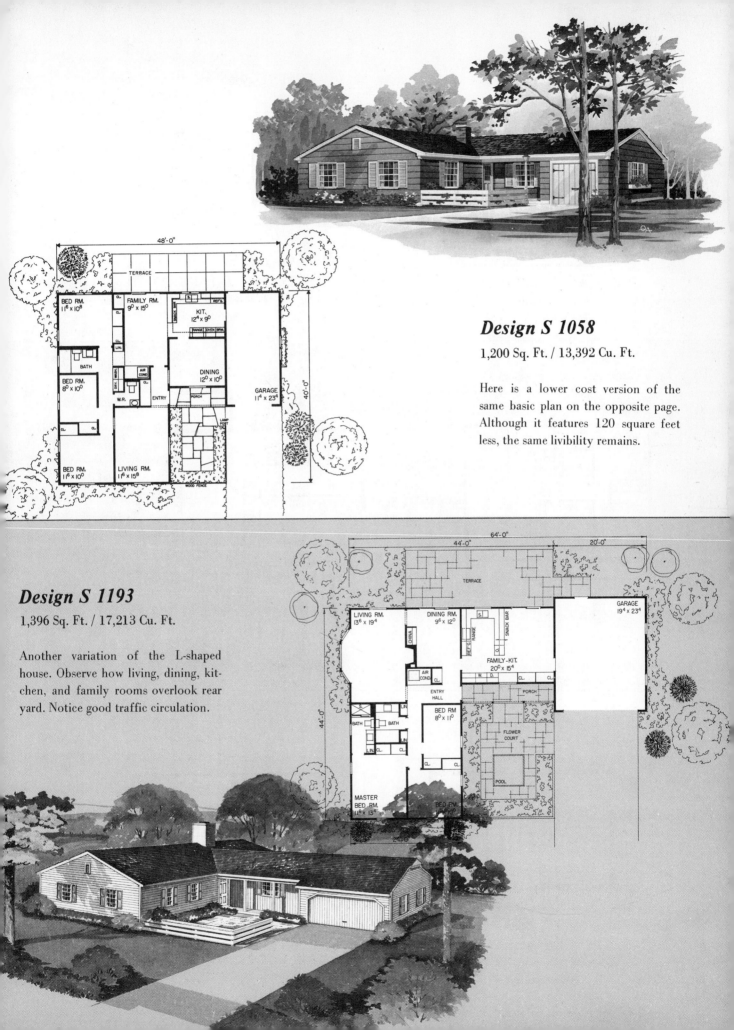

Design S 1058

1,200 Sq. Ft. / 13,392 Cu. Ft.

Here is a lower cost version of the same basic plan on the opposite page. Although it features 120 square feet less, the same livibility remains.

Design S 1193

1,396 Sq. Ft. / 17,213 Cu. Ft.

Another variation of the L-shaped house. Observe how living, dining, kitchen, and family rooms overlook rear yard. Notice good traffic circulation.

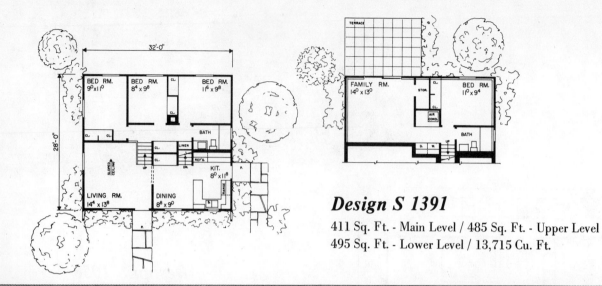

Design S 1391

411 Sq. Ft. - Main Level / 485 Sq. Ft. - Upper Level
495 Sq. Ft. - Lower Level / 13,715 Cu. Ft.

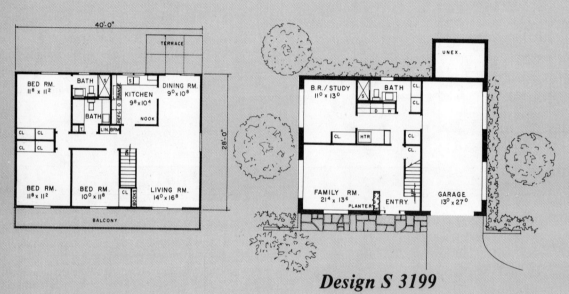

Design S 3199

1,120 Sq. Ft. - Lower Level / 728 Sq. Ft. - Upper Level
19,364 Cu. Ft.

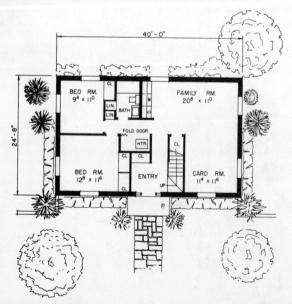

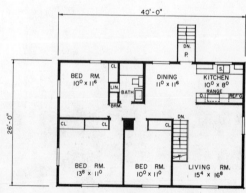

Design S 3198

986 Sq. Ft. - Lower Level / 1, 040 Sq. Ft. - Upper Level
20,368 Cu. Ft.

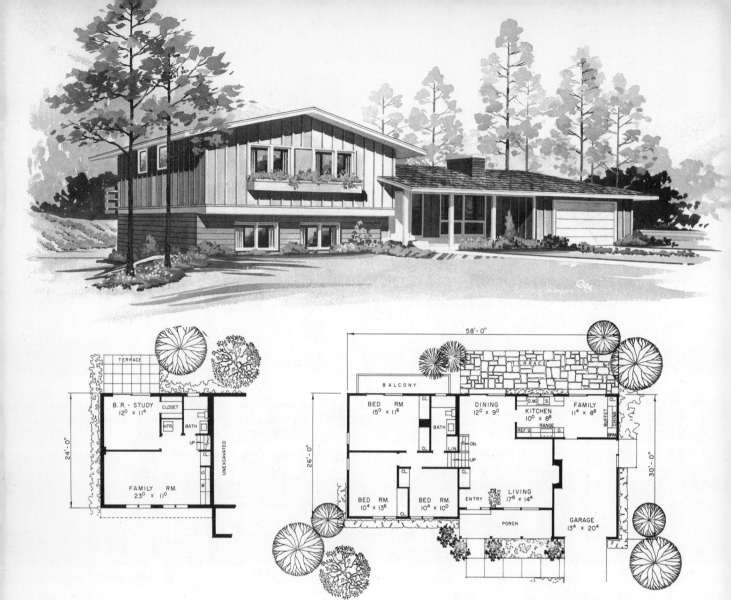

Design S 3217

612 Sq. Ft. - Main Level / 624 Sq. Ft. - Upper Level
576 Sq. Ft. - Lower Level / 17,911 Cu. Ft.

This is an exciting house. Each of the
three levels offers exceptional livability.
Count the extra features on each level.
The balcony will be popular.

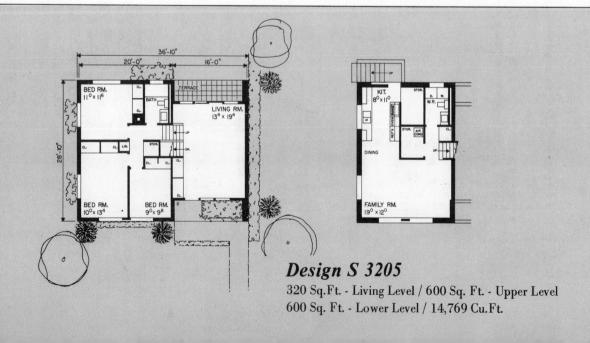

Design S 3205

320 Sq. Ft. - Living Level / 600 Sq. Ft. - Upper Level
600 Sq. Ft. - Lower Level / 14,769 Cu. Ft.

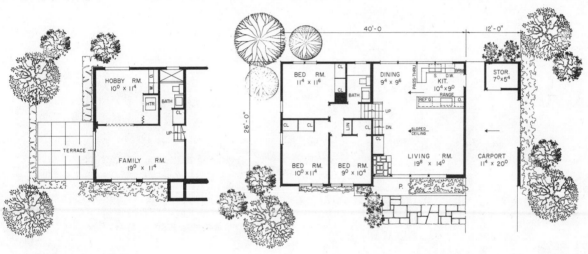

Design S 3216

488 Sq. Ft. - Main Level / 520 Sq. Ft. - Upper Level
480 Sq. Ft. - Lower Level / 15,822 Cu. Ft.

Contemporary tri-level living that will surely be fun for everyone. Don't miss the lower level family and hobby rooms, plus the extra full bath.

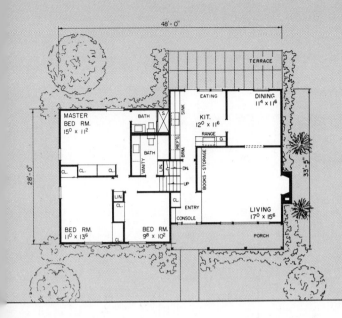

Design S 1112

686 Sq. Ft. - Main Level / 672 Sq. Ft. - Upper Level
336 Sq. Ft. - Lower Level / 19,132 Cu. Ft.

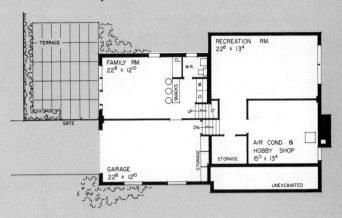

Design S 1353

484 Sq. Ft. - Main Level / 624 Sq. Ft. - Upper Level
300 Sq. Ft. - Lower Level / 13,909 Cu. Ft.

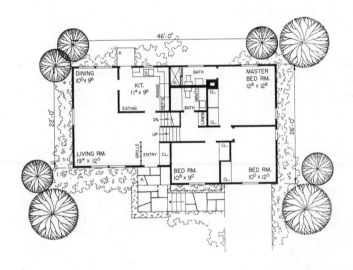

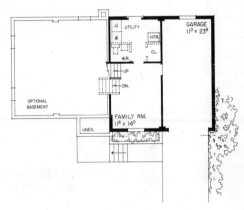

Design S 1386

880 Sq. Ft. - Upper Level
596 Sq. Ft. - Lower Level
14,043 Cu. Ft.

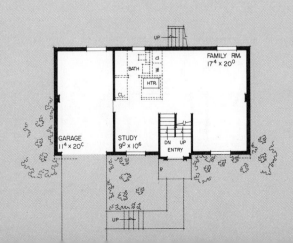

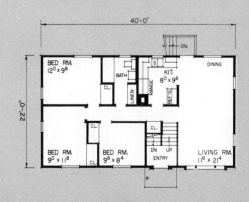

Design S 1719

864 Sq. Ft. - First Floor
896 Sq. Ft. - Second Floor
26,024 Cu. Ft.

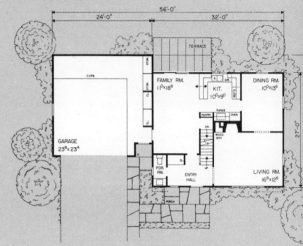

Design S 1913

740 Sq. Ft. - First Floor
728 Sq. Ft. - Second Floor
20,860 Cu. Ft.

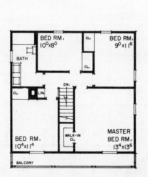

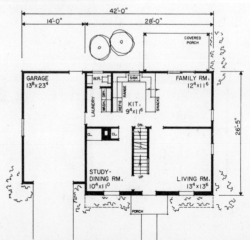

OPTIONAL NON-BASEMENT

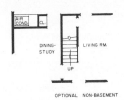

AIR COND. CL.

DINING- STUDY   LIVING RM.

UP

OPTIONAL NON-BASEMENT

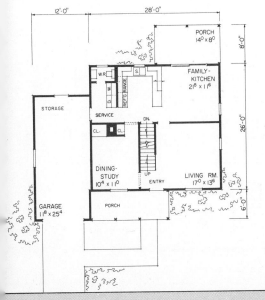

12'-0"   28'-0"

8'-0"

PORCH
14⁰ x 8⁰

FAMILY- KITCHEN
21⁸ x 11⁶

W.R.

S.

REF'G RANGE

D. W.

STORAGE

SERVICE

26'-0"

CL. CL.

DN.

UP

DINING- STUDY
10⁴ x 11⁰

ENTRY

LIVING RM.
17⁰ x 13⁶

GARAGE
11⁸ x 25⁴

PORCH

6'-0"

BED RM.
10⁰ x 8⁰

CL.

BED RM.
9⁰ x 11⁶

BATH

CL.

VANITY

CL.

LIN.

DN.

BED RM.
10⁴ x 11⁴

WALK-IN CL.

MASTER BED RM.
13⁴ x 13⁶

Design S 1368

728 Sq. Ft. - First Floor
728 Sq. Ft. - Second Floor
20,020 Cu. Ft.

Design S 1856

1,014 Sq. Ft. - First Floor
784 Sq. Ft. - Second Floor
25,570 Cu. Ft.

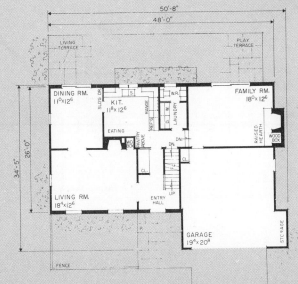

50'-8"

48'-0"

LIVING TERRACE

PLAY TERRACE

DINING RM.
11⁰ x 12⁶

SLDG DR

KIT.
11⁸ x 12⁶

S.

RANGE

REF'G

D. W.

W.R.

LAUNDRY

FAMILY RM.
18⁰ x 12⁶

EATING

PANTRY

ABOVE

PWD.

CL.

DN.

DN.

CL.

RAISED HEARTH

WOOD BOX

34'-5"

26'-0"

LIVING RM.
18⁴ x 12⁶

ENTRY HALL

UP

GARAGE
19⁴ x 20⁸

STORAGE

FENCE

MASTER BED RM.
15⁰ x 11⁶

BATH   BATH

CL.

CL. CL. CL.   LINEN

DN.

BED RM.
11⁴ x 13⁴

BED RM.
13⁴ x 10⁰

CL.

Design S 2118

915 Sq. Ft. - First Floor
864 Sq. Ft. - Second Floor
24,429 Cu. Ft.

The cedar shakes would make this Farmhouse adaptation at home on Cape Cod. Wherever built, whatever the exterior material, there's plenty of livability.

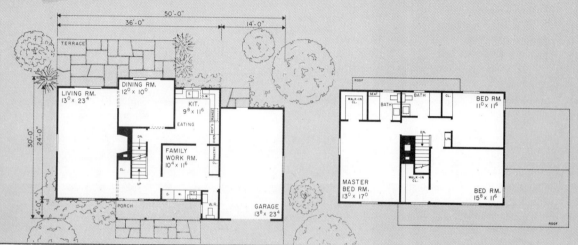

Design S 1354

644 Sq. Ft. - First Floor
572 Sq. Ft. - Second Floor
11,490 Cu. Ft.

Livability galore for that 50 foot building site. The homemaker will enjoy her U-shaped work center with the extra wash room, laundry equipment nearby.

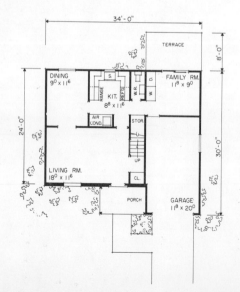

OPTIONAL BASEMENT

Design S 1361

965 Sq. Ft. - First Floor
740 Sq. Ft. - Second Floor
23,346 Cu. Ft.

All the elements are present in this design for fine family living. Three bedrooms, 2½ baths, family room, dining room, and even a first floor laundry.

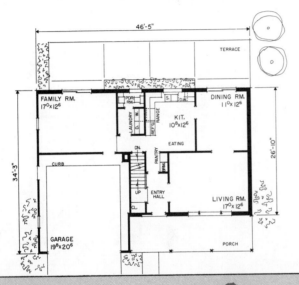

Design S 1723

888 Sq. Ft. - First Floor
970 Sq. Ft. - Second Floor
19,089 Cu. Ft.

You'll not need a large parcel of property to accommodate this home. Neither will you need too large a building budget. Note fourth bedroom.

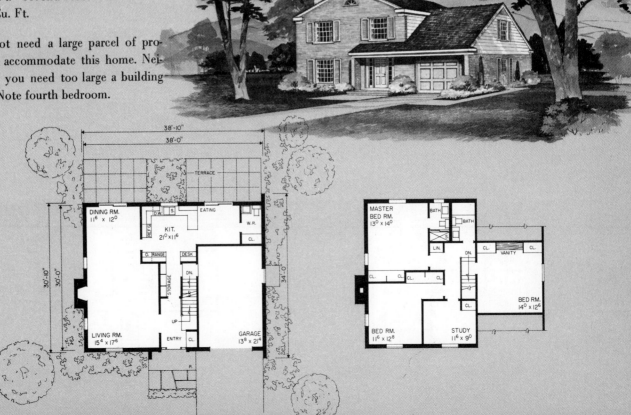

Design S 1365

952 Sq. Ft. - First Floor
574 Sq. Ft. - Second Floor
20,922 Cu. Ft.

This snug little story-and-a-half has three bedrooms, plus a study! It also has two baths, plus formal and informal dining areas.

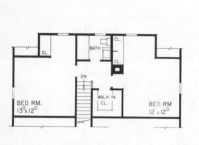

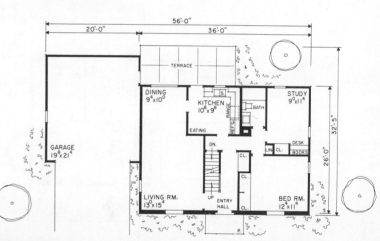

Design S 1372

768 Sq. Ft. - First Floor
432 Sq. Ft. - Second Floor
17,280 Cu. Ft.

Here is a vast amount of livability for the growing family. It will serve admirably for years to come. The upstairs may be finished later.

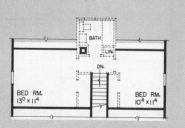

Design S 1791

1,157 Sq. Ft. - First Floor
875 Sq. Ft. - Second Floor
27,790 Cu. Ft.

Wherever you build this cozy house, an aura of Cape Cod is sure to unfold. The symmetry is pleasing, indeed; the livability is exceptional.

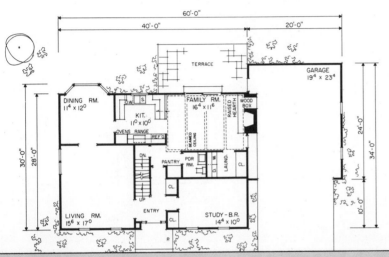

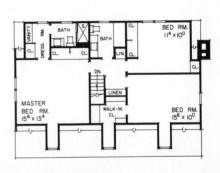

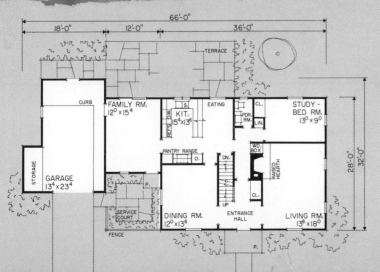

Design S 1901

1,200 Sq. Ft. - First Floor
744 Sq. Ft. - Second Floor
27,822 Cu. Ft.

Colonial charm could hardly be more appealingly captured than it is by this winsome design. The center entrance routes traffic most efficiently.

Design S 3189

884 Sq. Ft. - First Floor
444 Sq. Ft. - Second Floor
18,746 Cu. Ft.

Four bedrooms, two baths, a large kitchen-dining area, plenty of closets, a full basement, and an attached two-car garage are among the highlights here.

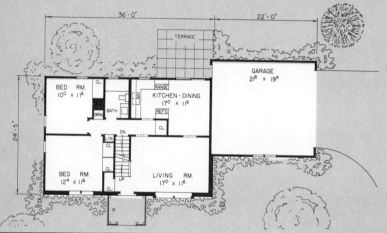

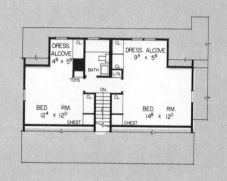

Design S 1394

832 Sq. Ft. - First Floor
512 Sq. Ft. - Second Floor
18,453 Cu. Ft.

Fine proportion and good design are not the exclusive property of huge houses. This little charmer will ably attest to that. Noteworthy is spacious living area.

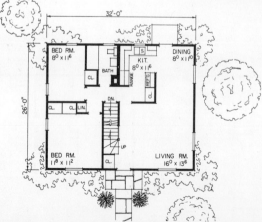

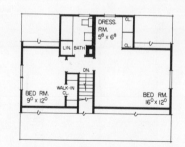

Design S 1870

1,136 Sq. Ft. - First Floor
936 Sq. Ft. - Second Floor
26,312 Cu. Ft.

Besides an enchanting exterior, this home has formal dining and living rooms, plus informal family and breakfast rooms. Note 2½ baths.

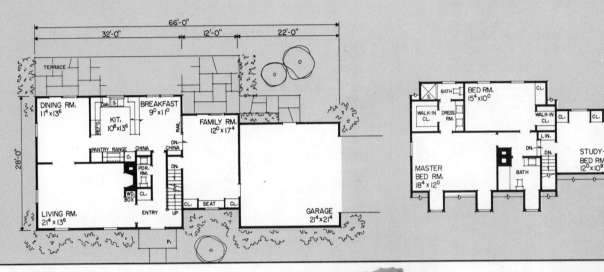

Design S 3126

1,141 Sq. Ft. - First Floor
630 Sq. Ft. - Second Floor
25,533 Cu. Ft.

Positively outstanding. From the delightful flower court to the upstairs storage room, this New England adaptation has much about which to talk.

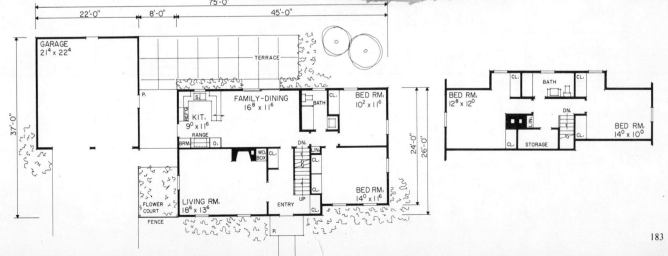

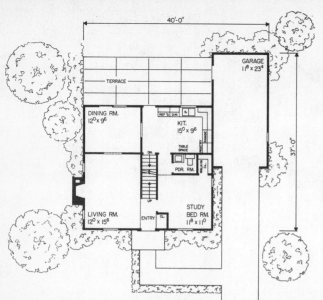

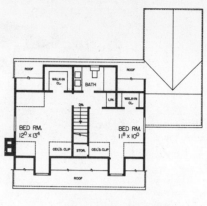

Design S 2162

728 Sq. Ft. - First Floor / 504 Sq. Ft. - Second Floor
17,895 Cu. Ft.

Design S 1196

1,008 Sq. Ft. - First Floor / 648 Sq. Ft. - Second Floor
23,884 Cu. Ft.

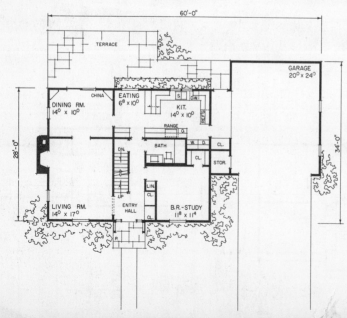

Design S 3135

880 Sq. Ft. - First Floor / 864 Sq. Ft. - Second Floor
23,980 Cu. Ft.

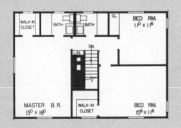

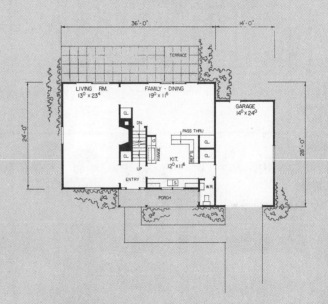

Design S 1318

854 Sq. Ft. - First Floor
896 Sq. Ft. - Second Floor
24,420 Cu. Ft.

For the large and growing family! Five bedrooms, 2½ baths, family room, separate dining rooms, efficient kitchen, full basement, and an attached garage.

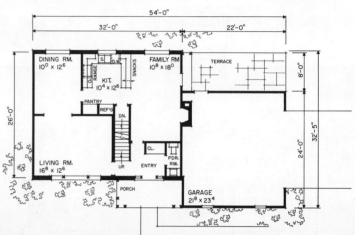

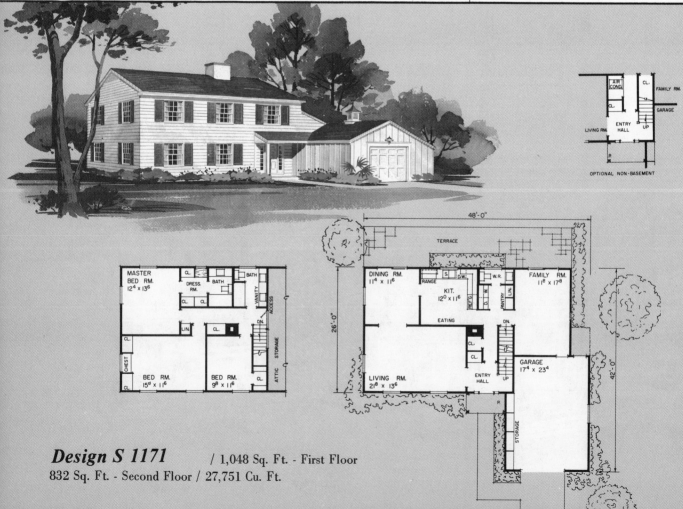

Design S 1171
/ 1,048 Sq. Ft. - First Floor
832 Sq. Ft. - Second Floor / 27,751 Cu. Ft.

Design S 1369

950 Sq. Ft. - First Floor
950 Sq. Ft. - Second Floor
27,550 Cu. Ft.

The stately columns of this home seem to belie its actual size. Imagine the spaciousness of the living area. Note the study and four bedrooms.

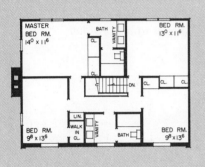

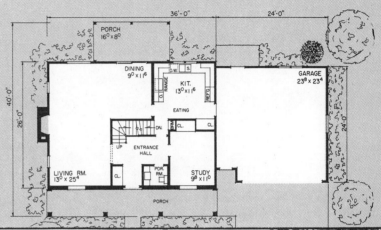

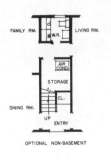

OPTIONAL NON-BASEMENT

Design S 1392   / 888 Sq. Ft. - First Floor

768 Sq. Ft. - Second Floor / 22,804 Cu. Ft.

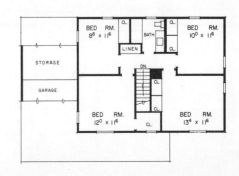

Here are three optional elevations that function with the same basic floor plan. No need to decide now which is your favorite since the blueprints for this design include details for each optional exterior.

If yours is a restricted building budget, your construction dollar could hardly return greater dividends in the way of exterior appeal and interior livability. Also, you won't need a big, expensive site on which to build.

In addition to the four bedrooms and 2½ baths, there are two living areas, two places for dining, a fireplace, and a basement. Notice the fine accessibility of the rear outdoor terrace.

Design S 2366

1,078 Sq. Ft.-First Floor
880 Sq. Ft.-Second Floor
29,557 Cu. Ft.

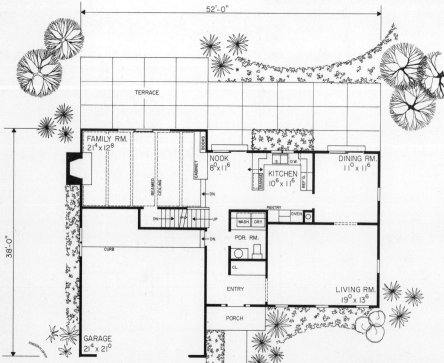

ALL THE "TOOLS" YOU & YOUR BUILDER NEED...

. . . to, first select an exterior and a floor plan for your new house that satisfy your tastes and your family's living patterns . . .
. . . then, to review the blueprints in great detail and obtain a construction cost figure . . . also, to price out the structural materials required to build . . . and, finally, to review and decide upon the specifications to which your home is to be built. Truly, an invaluable set of "tools" to launch your home planning and building programs.

1. THE PLAN BOOKS

Home Planners' unique Design Category Series makes it easy to look at and study only the types of designs for which you and your family have an interest. Each of five plan books features a specific type of home, namely: 1½ and 2-Story, One-Story *Over* 2000 Sq. Ft., One-Story *Under* 2000 Sq. Ft., Multi-Levels and Vacation Homes. Should you be undecided about the category of home you may want to build (any many of our readers are), the Complete Collection is available at a significant savings. Additional information about the availability of these books can be obtained directly from Home Planners, Inc., Dept. S 80, 23761 Research Dr., Farmington Hills, Michigan 48024.

2. THE CONSTRUCTION BLUEPRINTS

There are blueprints available for each of the designs published in Home Planners' current plan books. Depending upon the size, the style and the type of home, each set of blueprints consists of from five to ten large sheets. Only by studying the blueprints is it possible to give complete and final consideration to the proper selection of a design for your next home. The blueprints provide the opportunity for all family members to familiarize themselves with the features of all exterior elevations, interior elevations and details, all dimensions, special built-in features and effects. They also provide a full understanding of the materials to be used and/or selected. The low-cost of our blueprints makes it possible and indeed, practical, to study in detail a number of different sets of blueprints before deciding upon which design to build.

3. MATERIAL LIST

A list of materials is an integral part of the plan package. It comprises the last sheet of each set of blueprints and serves as a handy reference during the period of construction. Of course, at the pricing and the material ordering stages, it is indispensable.

4. THE SPECIFICATION OUTLINE

Each order for blueprints is accompanied by one Specification Outline. You and your builder will find this a time-saving tool when deciding upon your own individual specifications. An important reference document should you wish to write your own specifications.

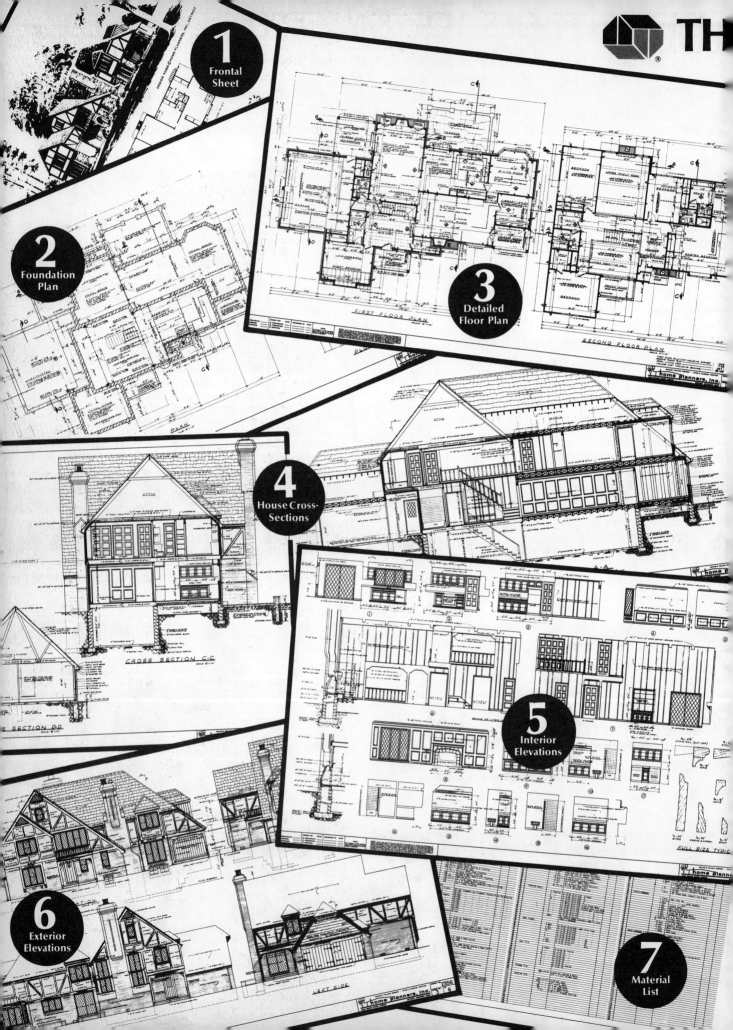

1 Frontal Sheet

2 Foundation Plan

3 Detailed Floor Plan

4 House Cross-Sections

5 Interior Elevations

6 Exterior Elevations

7 Material List

TH

BLUEPRINTS...

1. FRONTAL SHEET. Artist's landscaped sketch of the exterior and ink-line floor plans are on the frontal sheet of each set of blueprints.

2. FOUNDATION PLAN. 1/4" Scale basement and foundation plan. All necessary notations and dimensions. Plot plan diagram for locating house on building site.

3. DETAILED FLOOR PLAN. 1/4" Scale first and second floor plans with complete dimensions. Cross-section detail keys. Diagrammatic layout of electrical outlets and switches.

4. HOUSE CROSS-SECTIONS. Large scale sections of foundation, interior and exterior walls, floors and roof details for design and construction control.

5. INTERIOR ELEVATIONS. Large scale interior details of the complete kitchen cabinet design, bathrooms, powder room, laundry, fireplaces, paneling, beam ceilings, built-in cabinets, etc.

6. EXTERIOR ELEVATIONS. 1/4" Scale exterior elevation drawings of front, rear, and both sides of the house. All exterior materials and details are shown to indicate the complete design and proportions of the house.

7. MATERIAL LIST. Complete lists of all materials required for the construction of the house as designed are included in each set of blueprints.

THIS BLUEPRINT PACKAGE . . . will help you and your family take a major step forward in the final appraisal and planning of your new home. Only by spending many enjoyable and informative hours studying the numerous details included in the complete package, will you feel sure of, and comfortable with, your commitment to build your new home. To assure successful and productive consultation with your builder and/or architect, reference to the various elements of the blueprint package is a must. The blueprints, material list and specification outline will save much consultation time and expense. Don't be without them.

THE MATERIAL LIST...

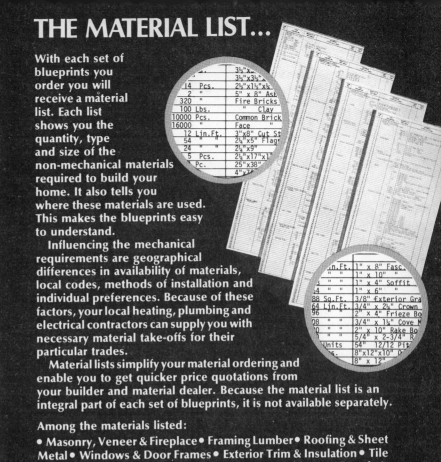

With each set of blueprints you order you will receive a material list. Each list shows you the quantity, type and size of the non-mechanical materials required to build your home. It also tells you where these materials are used. This makes the blueprints easy to understand.

Influencing the mechanical requirements are geographical differences in availability of materials, local codes, methods of installation and individual preferences. Because of these factors, your local heating, plumbing and electrical contractors can supply you with necessary material take-offs for their particular trades.

Material lists simplify your material ordering and enable you to get quicker price quotations from your builder and material dealer. Because the material list is an integral part of each set of blueprints, it is not available separately.

Among the materials listed:

• Masonry, Veneer & Fireplace • Framing Lumber • Roofing & Sheet Metal • Windows & Door Frames • Exterior Trim & Insulation • Tile Work, Finish Floors • Interior Trim, Kitchen Cabinets • Rough & Finish Hardware

THE SPECIFICATION OUTLINE...

This fill-in type specification lists over 150 phases of home construction from excavating to painting and includes wiring, plumbing, heating and air-conditioning. It consists of 16 pages and will prove invaluable for specifying to your builder the exact materials, equipment and methods of construction you want in your new home. One Specification Outline is included free with each order for blueprints. Additional Specification Outlines are available at $2.00 each.

CONTENTS

• General Instructions, Suggestions and Information • Excavating and Grading • Masonry and Concrete Work • Sheet Metal Work • Carpentry, Millwork, Roofing, and Miscellaneous Items • Lath and Plaster or Drywall Wallboard • Schedule for Room Finishes • Painting and Finishing • Tile Work • Electrical Work • Plumbing • Heating and Air-Conditioning

BEFORE YOU ORDER

1. STUDY THE DESIGNS . . . found in Home Planners current publications. As you review these delightful custom homes, you should keep in mind the total living requirements of your family — both indoors and outdoors. Although we do not make changes in plans, many minor changes can be made prior to the period of construction. If major changes are involved to satisfy your personal requirements, you should consider ordering one set of blueprints and having them redrawn locally. Consultation with your architect is strongly advised when contemplating major changes.

2. HOW TO ORDER BLUEPRINTS . . . After you have chosen the design that satisfies your requirements, or if you have selected one that you wish to study in more detail, simply clip the accompanying order blank and mail with your remittance. However, if it is not convenient for you to send a check or money order, you can use your credit card, or merely indicate C.O.D. shipment. Postman will collect all charges, including postage and C.O.D. fee. C.O.D. shipments are not permitted to Canada or foreign countries. Should time be of essence, as it sometimes is with many of our customers, your telephone order usually can be processed and shipped in the next day's mail. Simply call: (313) 477-1850.

3. OUR SERVICE . . . Home Planners makes every effort to process ship each order for blueprints and books *within 48 hours*. Becaus this, we have deemed it unnecessary to acknowledge receipt of our customers' orders. See order coupon below for the postage and hand charges for surface mail, air mail or foreign mail.

4. A NOTE REGARDING REVERSE BLUEPRINTS . . . As a special ser to those wishing to build in reverse of the plan as shown, we c include an extra set of reversed blueprints for only $15.00 additional w each order. Even though the lettering and dimensions appear backware reversed blueprints, they make a handy reference because they show house just as it's being built in reverse from the standard blueprints — thereby helping you visualize the home better.

5. OUR EXCHANGE POLICY . . . Since blueprints are printed up specific response to your individual order, we cannot honor reque for refunds. However, the first set of blueprints in any order (or the one se a single set order) for a given design may be exchanged for a set of anoth design at a fee of $10.00, plus $1.50 for postage and handling via surface ma $2.00 via air mail.

CLIP THIS COUPON AND MAIL TODAY!

TO: **HOME PLANNERS, INC., 23761 RESEARCH DRIVE FARMINGTON HILLS, MICHIGAN 48024**

Please rush me the following:

_____ SET(S) BLUEPRINTS FOR DESIGN NO(S). _____ $_____
Single Set $75.00, Additional Identical Sets in Same Order $15.00 ea.
(Material Lists and 1 Specification Outline included)
_____ SPECIFICATION OUTLINES @ $2.00 EACH . . . . $_____

Michigan Residents add 4% sales tax $_____

FOR POSTAGE AND HANDLING PLEASE CHECK ✔ & REMIT
☐ $1.50 Added to Order for Surface Mail — Any Mdse.
☐ $2.00 Added for Air Mail of One Set of Blueprints only.
☐ $3.00 Added for Air Mail of Two or more Sets of Blueprints only.
☐ For Foreign Mail add $2.00 to above applicable rates.
$_____

☐ C.O.D. PAY POSTMAN (C.O.D. Within U.S.A. Only) TOTAL in U.S.A. funds . . . $_____

Name _____
Street _____
City _____ State _____ Zip _____

Prices subject to change without notice

CREDIT CARD ORDER ONLY: Fill in the boxes below
Credit Card No. [ ][ ][ ][ ][ ][ ][ ][ ][ ][ ][ ][ ][ ][ ][ ][ ]
Expiration Date Month/Year [ ][ ][ ][ ]
CHECK ONE: ☐ VISA ☐ master charge
Master Charge Interbank No. [ ][ ][ ][ ]

Your Signature _____

S 80

TO: **HOME PLANNERS, INC., 23761 RESEARCH DRIVE FARMINGTON HILLS, MICHIGAN 48024**

Please rush me the following:

_____ SET(S) BLUEPRINTS FOR DESIGN NO(S). _____ $_____
Single Set $75.00, Additional Identical Sets in Same Order $15.00 ea.
(Material Lists and 1 Specification Outline included)
_____ SPECIFICATION OUTLINES @ $2.00 EACH . . . . $_____

Michigan Residents add 4% sales tax $_____

FOR POSTAGE AND HANDLING PLEASE CHECK ✔ & REMIT
☐ $1.50 Added to Order for Surface Mail — Any Mdse.
☐ $2.00 Added for Air Mail of One Set of Blueprints only.
☐ $3.00 Added for Air Mail of Two or more Sets of Blueprints only.
☐ For Foreign Mail add $2.00 to above applicable rates.
$_____

☐ C.O.D. PAY POSTMAN (C.O.D. Within U.S.A. Only) TOTAL in U.S.A. funds . . . $_____

Name _____
Street _____
City _____ State _____ Zip _____

Prices subject to change without notice

CREDIT CARD ORDER ONLY: Fill in the boxes below
Credit Card No. [ ][ ][ ][ ][ ][ ][ ][ ][ ][ ][ ][ ][ ][ ][ ][ ]
Expiration Date Month/Year [ ][ ][ ][ ]
CHECK ONE: ☐ VISA ☐ master charge
Master Charge Interbank No. [ ][ ][ ][ ]

Your Signature _____

S 80

In Canada Mail To: Home Planners, Inc., 772 King St. W., Kitchener, Ontario N2G IE8

HOW MANY SETS OF BLUEPRINTS SHOULD BE ORDERED?

This question is often asked. The answer can range anywhere from 1 to 8 sets, depending upon circumstances. For instance, a single set of blueprints of your favorite design is sufficient to study the house in greater detail. On the other hand, if you are planning to get cost estimates, or if you are planning to build, you may need as many as eight sets of blueprints. Because the first set of blueprints in each order is $75.00, and because additional sets of the same design in each order are only $15.00 each, you save considerably by ordering your total requirements now. To help you determine the exact number of sets, please refer to the handy check list below.

CHECK LIST FOR BLUEPRINTS . . . NUMBER OF SETS:

○ **OWNER'S SET**

○ **BUILDER** (Usually requires at least 3 sets: 1 as legal document; 1 for inspection; and at least 1 for tradesmen — usually more).

○ **FOR BUILDING PERMIT** (Sometimes 2 sets are required).

○ **MORTGAGE SOURCE** (Usually 1 set for conventional mortgage; 3 sets for F.H.A. or V.A. type mortgages).

○ **SUBDIVISION COMMITTEE** (If any)

○ **TOTAL NO. SETS REQUIRED**

ALL BLUEPRINT ORDERS SHIPPED WITHIN 48 HOURS!